# Uncomfortable but design.

## The events that changed the history of Design

Codice ISBN: 9798398083804

Author:

Matteo Bianchi

matteobianchi.it

OVERTHESIGN edizioni

# INDICE

# Design Unveiled:
# Exploring the Unknown.

When a simple object becomes 'Design'…?
A simple yet effective example explains it clearly.
Let's take an object that most of us are not very familiar with: a fisherman's pocket knife. If this object works really well, satisfies its user, and incorporates a small innovative utility compared to its predecessor, then it is a true design object. Functionality and innovation are essential characteristics in design, and if the object is also beautiful, that's even better, but it is a sufficient condition, not a necessary one. We must consider that the fisherman is not attending a fashion show by the river, and he doesn't need a pretty knife, but rather one that is useful and functional. That's it, nothing more and nothing less.
In confirmation of this, Bruno Munari, a great designer of the last century, said:

*"Design has nothing to do with beauty, luxury, or fashion. A design object is a beautiful product that works."*

The term 'design' is an English word which, simplifying its translation without betraying its concept, can be rendered in Italian as 'progetto' (project). The word 'progettare' (to design) derives from the Latin word 'proiectare,' which means 'to throw forward.' Therefore, it is not far-fetched to say that design means 'going beyond,' 'breaking a limit,' just as when one surpasses a constraint that is no longer valid.

Usually, it is believed that design is the study of an object's form, i.e., 'styling.' It is also commonly thought that a designer is a kind of artist, a creator of aesthetically 'cool' objects, often expensive. But this type of work is not just about giving structure to a casing: design is a combination that brings together technique, cognitive science, social aspects, expressive ability, technology, and elegant form to produce something that did not exist before. Therefore, we can assert that the figure that comes closest to the designer is that of the inventor.

However, it is necessary to establish some order in the realm of this discipline because it is not an easily delineated territory: an object in which the aesthetic component prevails over the functional one is not a design object but simply one that is not very (or not at all) effective. On the other hand, when function sacrifices aesthetics, the object in question more properly falls into the category of engineering rather than design.

Furthermore, if an object lacks both functionality and aesthetic qualities, then we are simply dealing with something that deserves the label of a 'poor product' that does not meet the users' needs or presents issues related to quality, usability, or safety.

Therefore, we can recognize design objects because they are characterized by well-balanced aspects that include innovation, functionality, and form (beauty), which plays an extremely important role, especially in our modern times. Enzo Mari stated that 'form is excellent when there are no alternatives...' meaning when perfection has been achieved.

But understanding whether the object in front of us satisfies these components is not a simple task. A true design object can pass by unnoticed: usually, we are more easily aware of ugly or poorly conceived objects than fully successful ones. To make a comparison, a design object is a bit like air conditioning in a closed environment: we only notice its presence or absence when it is too hot, too cold, when it makes too much noise, or when it drips on the floor. When the conditioning of an environment is perfect, there is no reason to be aware of it. Therefore, it is through usage that we grasp the real nature of the object; it is only by using it that we realize we can't do without it or that we can't take our eyes off it because it somehow makes us feel better.

In general, designers work to improve users' experience with a product by creating aesthetic and functional solutions that meet users' needs while respecting the client's requirements. It is perhaps due to this complex and composite nature that design also possesses something inevitably artistic. However, the separation between art and design is clear. Simply put, we can say that a designer must create a product that is useful, functional, and appealing to as many people as possible, while an artist doesn't have to worry too much about pleasing others but rather expresses themselves and their perception of the universe. Ultimately, creating design objects means making the world around us better by establishing a relationship between the product and the person who will use it, solving a real problem.

However, having a great intuition alone is not enough. If we think about it, we will certainly realize that all of us, at least once in our lives, have had a good idea, but in most cases, that idea was not carried out simply because we didn't know how to make it happen. This is particularly true in the field of design: reaching a finished object is a long and complex process that requires navigating technical and stylistic challenges, balancing the client's needs with those of the buyer. How does a designer accomplish all this? With technical skills, creativity, and observational spirit. The first can be learned at school, the second is partly innate and partly honed through diverse experiences, and finally, there is a need for a great deal of curiosity.

Indeed, the most capable designers observe everything around them because they are interested in objects, but even more so in the interactions these objects have with the people who will use them; they seek to address a need and create a comfortable sense of 'using that thing.' In them, the practical sense of an adult blends with a curiosity and a perspective that belong to the world of childhood, without generating any contradiction.

Some of them have succeeded in creating unforgettable objects, objects that still today, decades later, are part of our daily lives.

To truly understand how they achieved this, we would need to, paraphrasing Newton's words, 'stand on the shoulders of giants,' meaning to get as close as possible to the exact moment when the object in question was born, learning about it from the direct voice of its creator.

In this book, therefore, the stories of those men who, despite becoming giants, never stopped being children will be told.

# "The Stories of the "Giants"

*"The egg has a perfect shape,
even if it's laid from the ass."*

Bruno Munari

# Coffee Maker "Moka"
Alfonso Bialetti
BIALETTI 1933

In this incredible product, every choice serves a practical as well as aesthetic purpose; nothing is left to chance. The octagonal boiler ensures a comfortable grip even on wet surfaces, the handle and spout are made of Bakelite to withstand high temperatures, the inspectable valve, filter, and gasket allow for easy closure. Today, almost 80 years after its creation, it has remained virtually unchanged.

# Renato, I've never had such a good coffee before...

**A quality product represents only a piece of commercial success; the rest depends on an enlightened entrepreneur, effective investment, communicative marketing, and an efficient sales network..**

The Moka Bialetti is undoubtedly the most important symbol of Italian coffee culture. In fact, 90% of Italian households own at least one, and many homes have them in various sizes.

The story begins in 1919 when Alfonso Bialetti founded a foundry in Crusinallo, which bore his name. However, due to financial problems, he had to sell it to his father-in-law, Giovanni Alessi, in 1927. Giovanni Alessi went on to establish the famous homeware company that still bears his name today.

In the early 1930s, Alfonso had a brilliant idea while watching his wife doing the laundry. The precursor to the washing machine was called a "lisciveuse," which was a container with a steel tube in the center. The laundry was placed in the tube, and when the water reached boiling point, it would rise through the tube, distributing the soap more evenly.

This technique sparked Alfonso Bialetti's imagination as he envisioned a creative method to make coffee preparation faster and easier. In the early 1900s, the prevailing method was "percolation," where 2 tablespoons of coffee were infused in boiling water and then filtered.

Then came the Napoletana, a somewhat dangerous coffee maker that involved flipping it over once the water started boiling.

Alfonso began working on his idea, and although the coffee maker in 1933 was not the same as the one we use today, the base was somewhat stubby, maintaining the octagonal shape that made opening and closing the coffee maker easy, even with slightly damp hands. Additionally, the handle and knob were made of wood.

During those years, Bialetti created the first "Moka Express" with a square design featuring geometric lines reminiscent of Art Deco. However, the shape was actually derived from a shell mold made in two openable pieces used for pouring the molten metal and not necessarily influenced by that particular style.

For the material, Alfonso chose aluminum, which was very popular at that time. It was the metal symbol of the Fascist dictatorship and highly favored by the Futurist artists. Aluminum was used to produce airplanes, and it was fast, resistant, unattackable, satin-finished, and could be colored or mirror-polished like silver. Alfonso believed aluminum was perfect because the calcium present in the water would remain at the bottom, while the upper part, where the coffee emerges, would absorb its essence over time, resulting in an even more intense aroma.

However, it's not entirely true that the Moka should not be washed. The reason for not washing it is simply that there is a space between the spout and the filter that is not reachable and could be soiled with soap, leaving residues in the boiling mixture.

In 1933, Bialetti reopened the company and produced his Moka, claiming it made "espresso like at the bar." Keep in mind that until that moment, coffee was primarily made in coffee bars, and the Moka made it convenient to have it at home upon waking up. Between 1936 and 1940, Alfonso personally sold his product at markets and fairs, selling about 50,000 units, which was a small number, and the product didn't take off.

Alfonso was essentially a technician who, with a cigar in his mouth in the evenings, pondered over poorly made pieces. He was not an effective entrepreneur.

The turning point for success came thanks to his son Renato, who returned from a labor camp in Germany after the war and took over the company in 1946. He removed the protective covers placed by his father on the machinery and set up a new workshop capable of producing 18,000 coffee makers per day, 4 million per year. It is estimated that over 300 million coffee makers have been produced in 77 years. [1]

Renato focused mainly on promoting the Moka through large city billboards and magazine articles. However, the real boom came with the television advertising campaign called *Carosello*. Renato decided to invest in advertising to increase sales. The brand became well-known thanks to the mascot named

---

[1] Il Sole 24 Ore: 'History of Bialetti, from the Moka boom to the red balance sheets.

"l'Omino con i Baffi" (the Little Man with Mustache), a caricature of Renato with his finger raised as if ordering coffee. This logo is still imprinted on original coffee makers today. Renato's entrepreneurial skills, combined with his significant investment in advertising and communication, paid off. Sales skyrocketed, imprinting the image of the mustachioed Little Man in the minds of Italians, with a versatile mouth that transformed into the shapes of spoken letters. He used to say, *"It seems easy... to make good coffee."*

In 1986, Renato, elderly by then, sold the highly successful company (with an annual turnover of 20 billion) to Faema. He passed away in 2016, and as per his wishes, his ashes were collected in a giant Moka [2]. However, there is an anecdote I want to share. In an interview, Renato revealed a little-known story. He said that he was helped in sales by the Greek billionaire Aristotle Onassis. Here are his words from the interview: *"I was in a hotel with French clients, and the coffee maker was almost a novelty for them. They were hesitant and doubtful, and I realized they wouldn't close the deal. At that moment, Aristotle Onassis, the Greek billionaire, passed by close to us. He was heading towards the bathroom. Without thinking twice, I gathered up my courage and followed him. I said, 'Hello, Mr. Onassis, I'm a young Italian entrepreneur, just like you, who started from nothing. Please help me. When you return to the lobby, tell them you use my coffee maker. I need to make an impression on these reluctant French clients.' I went back, convinced and resigned that Onassis would simply carry on. But then, a miracle*

---

2 Funeral of Bialetti, the entrepreneur's ashes in a Moka, on Corriere.it

*happened. Onassis, pretending to see me at the last moment, turned back, patted me on the shoulder, and said, 'Renato, how are you? Do you know I've never had such a good cup of coffee as the one from your coffee maker?"* [3] It was an incredible success. Alfonso (the father) conceived it, and Renato (the son) made it known worldwide.

Without either of them, the Moka probably wouldn't be in our homes today because genius without entrepreneurial vision doesn't sell, and commercial strength without an innovative and functional product doesn't make progress.

In conclusion, I leave you with Renato's own words: *"With a strong advertising campaign. At that time, after the war, advertising was a novelty. The product launch was made possible thanks to Carosello and the Mustachioed Little Man, which was my caricature created by my good friend Paul Campani, the screenwriter who created Carosello. Italians loved it. And besides, the coffee was really good, as even Onassis said..."*

---

3  Taken from an article in *La Stampa*. Renato Bialetti: 'That's how Onassis pretended to be my customer"

# Coffè Table "Lovet"
Ingvar Kamprad
IKEA 1956

LÖVET remained in the IKEA catalog until 1962. It was in 2013 that product developer Glenn Berndtsson proposed to Ingvar Kamprad to examine old documents of beautiful products that could be given new life. The decision was made to recreate several classic furniture pieces from the 1950s and '60s, including the iconic LÖVET table.

*Glenn said, "The side table has been designed to closely resemble the original. Put two of them together, side by side, and it's impossible to spot the difference."*

# "F**K you...<br>if it doesn't fit in the car<br>now, I'll break its legs."

**A successful product must be innovative, functional, attractive, and accessible. Optimizing production processes can lead to significant advantages. It is important to conduct thorough market research and maintain effective communication with the production team and sales network.**

Ingvar Kamprad, at the age of 17, founded what we all know as Ikea in 1943. Initially, the items sold were small objects such as pens, wallets, and picture frames. Only a few years later, he started selling furniture by mail order. The exact birthplace of Ikea is Älmhult, a town in a remote area of Sweden. Since reaching customers in large cities was not easy, the first Ikea catalog was born in 1951, an ideal commercial "tool" to be sent to all potential customers.

In 1953, Ikea hired its fourth employee, Gillis Lundgren, who was responsible for the company's graphics and furniture photography. There is a curious story involving the Lovet leaf table. One day, while loading the table into the car trunk to take it to the photography studio, despite trying in every way to fit it in fully assembled, he made the discovery that the table simply wouldn't fit. Frustrated, he exclaimed, *"Now I'll saw off your legs, and let's see if you fit, you darn thing!"*

Then he stopped and realized that from a certain perspective, sawing off the legs or simply removing four screws to disassemble it was much more convenient. He put his idea into action and soon realized that transporting furniture in a disassembled state was much more practical. He didn't stop at just one consideration. In fact, shortly after, he realized that this operation brought significant economic advantages.

The furniture could be packed flat, individually packaged with cardboard and twine—this was the commercial message of the time. There were many reasons in favor of this choice. Customer assembly saved a lot of money, and moreover, the furniture arrived intact without any dents, as often happened with shipments of fully assembled furniture.

The owner of Ikea, Ingvar Kamprad, realized that in the future, the company's savings and profits could come from a new concept regarding product assembly and distribution. This last point was crucial to Ikea's success.

After careful consideration, he decided to embrace the suggestion of his fourth employee, Lundgren, and entrusted him with designing furniture suitable for shipping and easy assembly. Lundgren, filled with enthusiasm, discussed this during lunch in the cafeteria with his colleague, Billy Liljedahl, and asked which furniture he should design first. Billy responded, *"A proper bookcase."*

Lundgren said at the time, *"I sketched the first designs on a napkin right there on the spot. That was often how we worked. Ideas are perishable, and you*

*have to capture the moment as soon as it comes.*" [4]
So he immediately got to work and created the most
famous piece of furniture in Ikea's history that is still
popular today—the "Billy" bookcase.

The first IKEA store in Stockholm in 1965

[4] Taken from an interview with Gillis Lundgren, designer of the "Billy"
bookcase at IKEA (web furniturehomewares.com)

# Wall Clock "4755-Clock Ball"
### elson, Harper, Noguchi, Fuller. (Maybe...)
### MILLER CLOCK CO. 1947

This wall clock model doesn't have numbers surrounding the dial, but instead it has spheres indicating the hour positions. In its first version, it had a brass center from which 12 equal brass spokes radiated, with painted wooden balls at their ends. This 1947 model was the first of over 130 clocks designed by George Nelson Associates for the Howard Miller Clock Company.

# «"Come on, move aside...! How much have you been drinking??"»

**It is an extraordinary achievement to transform established forms over time into designs that offer new functionalities, combining innovative and functional aesthetics.**

It is an extraordinary achievement to transform established forms over time into designs that offer new functionalities, combining innovative and functional aesthetics.

In any given project, when you bring together two designers, an engineer, and an artist, what will emerge is unknown to everyone, including themselves. The wall clock that has made history in design conceals a secret: it is not known exactly who conceived it.

George Nelson is considered one of the greatest exponents of American modernism, often referred to as "The creator of things that are not only beautiful but also practical." With his ingenuity, he successfully changed product design, graphic design, and interior design throughout his remarkable fifty-year career.

Nelson was an excellent creative and over the years, he shared moments of sudden inspiration that he experienced, which he called "creative zaps": *"When you suddenly discover that you are connected to a reality you never dreamed of, you become so engrossed in the idea that those around you imagine you're having a brain stroke..."*

A person of great talent, he founded his New York studio, George Nelson Associates, in 1947, and for the next twenty-five years, he and his colleague Irving Harper collaborated together, designing hundreds of products. Among the many companies they worked for, they collaborated with the Howard Miller Clock Company, creating over 130 wall clocks between 1949 and the mid-1980s. The first and most famous among them was the Ball Clock (Model 4755), the world's first wall clock without numbers.

In a 1953 interview, Nelson shared the story of how the ball clock came to life during a long and joyful night spent with friends. Nelson and Harper were still in the office when his friends Isamu Noguchi, a skilled sculptor, and Richard Buckminster Fuller, the brilliant inventor of geodesic domes, passed by. Regarding the conception of the wall clock, Nelson said:

*"I remember it was one of the most fun evenings. There was me, Irving, and then Noguchi came along with Bucky Fuller, and we had a couple of bottles of good wine. Pencils scratched on the translucent drafting paper, accompanied by laughter, jokes, and the popping of cork".* These men were also good partygoers. They say 'Bucky' was even expelled from Harvard for his excessive parties. Nelson continued: *"Noguchi, who can't keep his hands away from*

*anything, saw that we were working on clocks and started doodling on a sheet. Then Bucky pushed Isamu aside and said, 'Move over, this is how you make a clock...' and made an absolutely absurd scribble. At that point, everyone started pushing each other aside and scribbling. At some point, we left, as we were all tired and had definitely had a bit too much to drink. The next morning, we came back, and there it was, the sketch of the 'Ball Clock' on the sheet of paper on the table... Irving and I looked at it, and somewhere in that sheet, a ball clock was drawn. Even today, I don't know who actually came up with it..."* [5]

In his book titled "The Design of Modern Design," Nelson states that the project unmistakably bears the characteristics of Harper's imagination, Noguchi's creativity, and Fuller's engineering ability, and he is only certain about one thing: he didn't create it himself. Someone else had a timely "creative zap" (perhaps also fueled by alcohol) that night.

In this particular object, Nelson had the ingenuity to observe how people used clocks, and he concluded that they read the time by distinguishing the respective positions of the hands. This observation made the use of numbers marginal. Furthermore, considering that most people regularly wore wristwatches, he assumed that wall clocks had become, given the times, a decorative element that was part of the interior.

A great insight for a great project.

---

[5] The statement by George Nelson is excerpted from an interview conducted by Ralph Caplan in January 1981."

# Citrus Juicer "Juicy Salif"
Philippe Starck
ALESSI 1988

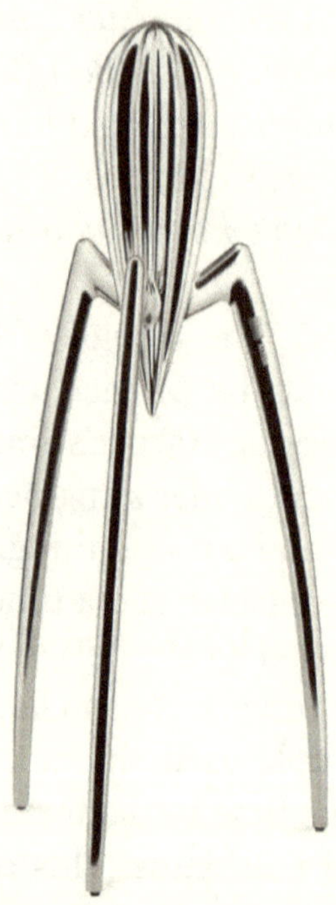

A citrus juicer made from a single piece of mirror-polished aluminum. The shape resembles that of an octopus with a body and 3 tentacles. The declared innovation is the complete absence of a container, instead, a glass is placed where the squeezed juice (with the seeds, unfortunately) is poured inside.

# "Excuse me, where can I spit the seeds?"

**A design product is a useful object that incorporates a significant innovative and functional feature, which helps users achieve a purpose without compromises. The task of a designer is to create objects that are truly useful, rather than objects that simply occupy space in the home without a clear purpose.**

Great ideas have always arisen from a need, a requirement that stimulates creativity. We find ourselves in the 1980s, on a hot summer day, sitting at a table in the Il Corsaro restaurant on the island of Capraia. There sits a man eagerly awaiting his ordered dish of baby octopus in sauce. This man is no ordinary man, but Philippe Starck, a true genius of contemporary design. When his plate of baby octopus is served, he notices the absence of lemon. In that moment of waiting, he begins to think of a brilliant idea with citrus juice as the main subject.

As often happens with tales of flashes of genius, the story of the citrus juicer also stems from a need. While still sitting at the table, the designer starts sketching on the paper placemat underneath the plate of baby octopus. The doodle resembles a sort of mollusk with tentacles. Several months later, a package arrives on

Alberto Alessi's desk (owner of Alessi, a renowned household goods manufacturer). Inside is a copy of the paper placemat where the designer had made his sketch. The drawing portrays the shape of what would later become the Juicy Salif citrus juicer. Alberto Alessi recognizes its expressive power and shortly after decides to put it into production, a production that has never ceased since that day.

Alberto Alessi, when interviewed about the citrus juicer, affirmed that not only did he consider it the most controversial object of the 20th century, but also one of the wittiest, charming, intelligent, and dare I say, provocative objects in the entire Alessi catalog. This object has managed to divide the opinions of many designers. Some see it as an example where form surpasses functionality, while others assert with reasonable certainty that it doesn't work all that well, considering that during the juicing process, the seeds, lacking a collection point, end up in the glass, requiring a second refinement to obtain pure juice.

Regarding design, one may question if it aligns with the term. It can certainly be defined as a sculptural object due to its original lines and the contrast with all the other citrus juicers deemed "classic." This object is somewhat the best emblem of that tenuous boundary between art and design that design sometimes traverses. Juicy Salif represents the epitome of the "uncomfortable object" that is still used even at the expense of its functionality. It is not the only one; there are many that populate our homes, perhaps awaiting the fateful question: 'It's beautiful, but what is it?'

Philippe Starck has managed to find an elegant way out by stating that Juicy Salif is NOT a classic citrus juicer but rather an incongruous 'object of conversation,' echoing Umberto Eco: *'This audacious citrus juicer is a somewhat wasted object because its dwelling is not the kitchen but the living room, where it can capture the attention of guests.'* In this case, the function of the object takes a backseat and is twofold. If one desires a classic citrus juicer, it may not be the ideal choice. However, if one desires an object with a distinct decorative function, with the ability to engage in an entertaining conversation, Juicy Salif is perfect.

As for the question of whether it is design or not...? The answer depends solely on one factor that answers this question: *'What do we really want?' Kitchen or living room? "*.

It solely depends on us.

This monumental coat rack is made of soft polyurethane, and each piece is unique as its 2165 protrusions are hand-finished. Furthermore, to ensure a durable and elastic surface, it is coated with multiple layers of a special paint called Guflac®, a secret recipe by Gufram, which protects it over time. The uniqueness of this object lies in the fact that it is still produced today using the original mold from 1972.

# "Guidoooooo, close the window, we're not in Hawaii!!!"

**Starting from the 1960s, practically every product has been influenced by the aesthetic remodeling processes generated by design. At some point, there was a felt need to embrace a creativity oriented towards aesthetics, towards what is beautiful, unique, and capable of eliciting emotions, going beyond mere functionality.**

Gufram is a furniture company founded by the Gugliermetto brothers in 1957, known primarily for its influence in the field of industrial design but also for actively contributing to revolutionizing furniture aesthetics from the 1960s onwards. It is recognized worldwide for pushing the boundaries of industrial design to some extent.

With its Radical Design spirit (see further in the History of Design), Gufram, through its aesthetic, technological, and material experiments, has managed to conceive and create seating and furnishings that have become part of the collective imagination. They can be defined as subversive products, simultaneously irreverent to the Pop spirit, conceived and intended as elements of anti-design. The company, born within the industrial fabric of the city of Turin, skillfully combines international artistic avant-gardes, producing true design icons since 1966. These creations take shape through a contamination of industrial and artisanal design approaches, along with the inherent inspiration of art itself.

They are often referred to as domestic sculptures, capable of combining the worlds of art and design, such as the famous Bocca sofa, the Pratone chaise longue, where giant petals manage to make us experience what a small ant feels, and finally, the Cactus coat rack. These objects have become part of the furnishings of many homes or have entered renowned museums due to their beauty combined with originality.

The Gufram Cactus coat rack was designed in 1972 by Guido Drocco in collaboration with Franco Mello. This object possesses numerous characteristics that make it unique. Firstly, it is a lively and highly original project, fully representing the creative atmosphere of the 1970s. Gufram, in its complete reinterpretation of Pop icons, colors it green and produces it in a scale suitable for interior environments. The Cactus landscape is irreverent, playful, ironic, and radical. Drocco and Mello work on a human-sized, soft, four-armed cactus: a coat rack that becomes a cheerful "domestic character," almost like a friend waiting for our return home, bringing a smile to our face. Drocco recounts that this story begins with the Gufram of the Gugliermetto brothers. In fact, they are the true protagonists of Italian Radical Design, and through their collaboration with the avant-garde movement in Turin, they succeeded in creating creations with irreverent, provocative, and playful designs.

These are their words, taken from an interview with Guido Drocco by Francesca Bolino of *Repubblica* in 2021: *"For us, back then, 'Design' meant conceiving objects born out of real needs. And this is the story of the Cactus. It was the winter of '71. I still lived in the small apartment on Via Sacchi in Turin. It was very cold outside, one of those dreary days: there was thick fog enveloping the whole city, and everything looked gray as I looked out the window. And it was at that moment that I desired to escape; I dreamed of exotic landscapes… I thought of an object that would evoke warm lands bathed in sunlight. I traced the initial sketches on a blank sheet of paper, but the project also came to life thanks to the help of Franco Mello and the suggestions of the artist and friend Piero Gilardi. We saw a sound-absorbing foam panel in a construction store, full of protrusions that perfectly conveyed the external appearance I was seeking for the cactus. It was Giuseppe Gugliermetto, with Gufram, who believed in us, and that's when the long trials with various materials began, followed by the issue of finishing, which was solved with the robust 'Guflac' coating, a pride of the Gugliermetto brothers. And so, the story of this important piece of home furnishing began. It was born by chance because I simply wanted a connection with nature and the sun, precisely because I was confined in a room."*

**_Sugar Bowl_ "Model n. 247"**
Christopher Dresser
ELKINGTON 1885

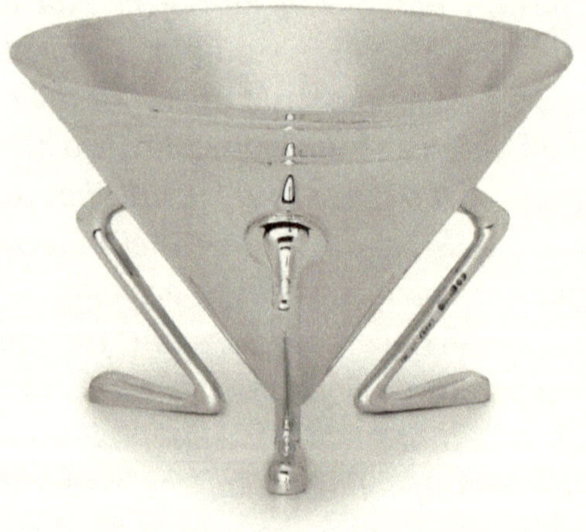

This particular model is a silver-plated sugar bowl whose ambiguous shape, upon closer analysis, reveals surprising ergonomic and functional details.

# "Chris, the sugar bowl with the elf-like legs looks beautiful."

**In the history of design, the shape of objects has always been a subject of debate and heated discussions. There has been discussion about whether the form should be mere decoration, minimalist, exaggerated, provocative, or strictly functional.**

Initially, the shape served merely as a casing to highlight the object, but over time it became elegant or surprising, exaggerated or minimal. It is only in relatively modern times that it is affirmed that the best possible shape is one that follows function, meaning that the form of an object should primarily concern its function with a minimal appearance. Many designers have expressed famous phrases on the concept of form. The most well-known remains that of Mies van der Rohe: *'Less is more,'* or even more clearly, 'less is better.' In contrast, there is the statement by the postmodern American architect Robert Venturi, 'Less is bore,' and many others expressing their idea of form.Considered by many historians as Europe's first professional industrial designer, Christopher Dresser, born in 1834 in Glasgow, Scotland, designed numerous innovative objects in his fifty-year career. One of these is the 247, a silver-plated sugar bowl, using an innovative technique of the time that allowed embellishing an object made of brass, a humble material, by electroplating it with a thin layer of silver, making it appear entirely solid silver. Maximum output, minimum expense.Dresser's product responded to an innovative thought in design, minimalist yet reasoned and planned for mass industrial production. Unsatisfied with the small handles that were attached to sugar bowls, which required people to insert their thumbs inside the rim to grip them properly, Dresser decided to experiment with a new shape. Since he believed that a cone was the most suitable form for a container of this type, as it facilitated separating powdered sugar from lumps, Dresser devised three little feet that would simultaneously support the cone's structure while also serving as handles.It was a project with careful study of form, where the elements of legs and body were designed for a specific function. Nothing was left to chance; everything was reduced to maximum simplicity. Numerous sketches by Dresser testify to his meticulous study of an object. Here, undoubtedly, he carefully studied the movement of the hand when grasping the sugar bowl and finally found the perfect solution in three slender shaped metal rods. What emerged was a very distinctive form.It amuses me to imagine someone passing by Dresser's worktable, perhaps his wife, looking at the drawing and saying, '*Nice, Chris, I like the little elf with frog-like legs you made, but now wash your hands, or the dinner will get cold.*' Christopher would have sighed, feeling diminished by the fleeting judgment devoid of any technical signance, disregarding all his studies on ergonomics and incapable of explaining his design motivations to his spouse for the hundredth time. He would have walked away from the drawing table to go to the bathroom and wash his hands as advised by his wife. Attention, it's not over yet, let's jump ahead a century. In the early 90s, Alessi, the well-known Italian household objects manufacturer, launched a project titled FFF (Family Follow Fiction), paraphrasing Louis Sullivan's famous axiom 'Form Follows Function.' For Alessi, the family became the subject, the home the place of reunion, and the guiding thread a joyful tale of fantasy. The team of designers convened by Alberto Alessi told a fable with anthropomorphic flavor, where objects became characters, actors in a scenic 'fiction,' narrators of relational stories. The objects on the table for the first time became a series of small creatures capable of evoking genuine emotions within the walls of the home. Someone on the Alessi team remembered Dresser's sugar bowl, capturing its playful trait, and in 1993, along with a series of colorful and fun objects (the emergence of Play Design, as we will see later in the history of design), they reproduced Dresser's container identically but made it in colored plastic, renaming it Christy in memory of its creator.

Dresser's wife would have said, *'I told you it looked like an elf, but you never listen... (come to the table; dinner is getting cold. This house is not a hotel).'*

Armchair **"Sacco"**
Gatti, Paolini,Teodoro
ZANOTTA 1969

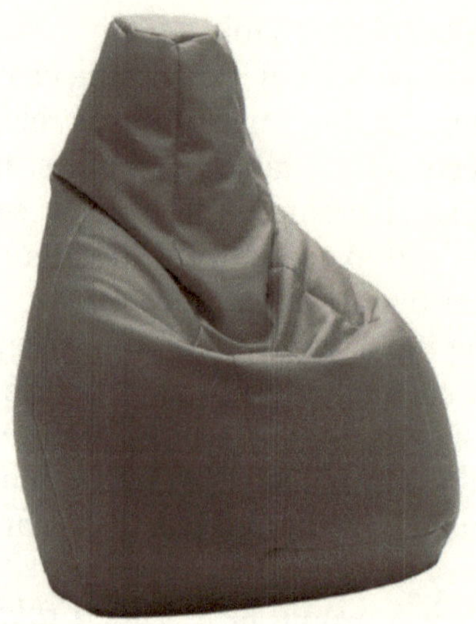

The Sacco armchair is a completely 'deconstructed' armchair, without legs and without a rigid backrest, a seat
that interacts with its user, changing its shape with every
movement.

# "Please, have a seat on my scrotum."

**There have been occasions when we have come across seemingly ordinary objects, exclaiming, "I could have done that too." However, the realization of such objects requires in-depth study, based on keen observation, critical thinking, and extensive technical expertise.**

Emilio Ambasz was an Argentine-American architect and award-winning industrial designer. From 1969 to 1976, he served as the Curator of the Design Department at MoMA in New York. He selected Sacco for the exhibition 'The New Italian Landscape' in 1972 and said about Sacco: *'It is a seat, an armchair, a small sofa, a chaise longue—it is whatever you want it to be because when you settle into it, your body remains somewhat suspended. When the shape formed by the weight starts to reassert itself, you simply need to change your position gently or give it a little punch to rough it up a bit and regain the sensation of lightness. It is a never-before-seen product.'*

Towards the end of the 1960s, three architects from Turin—Cesare Paolini, Piero Gatti, and Franco Teodoro—presented a prototype of a seat to Aurelio Zanotta, a forward-thinking furniture entrepreneur deeply fascinated by a certain nonconformism prevalent in the cultural and artistic trends of those years. He was certainly the first to bet on the importance of lines and subsequent experimentation with forms, which marked the true starting point of Italian design in the modern era.

These three architects carried on their shoulders a transparent plastic sack filled with polystyrene balls and proposed it as a 'seat.' *To achieve the desired softness, 'like the snow where one throws oneself and leaves the shape of one's body,'* they experimented with different materials such as water, air, and plastic toy bullets, but they didn't work. Then, the breakthrough came with polystyrene balls—small, soft, white balls the size of coffee beans. Modular, lightweight, and inexpensive.

The illuminating idea came from experiments with materials used for sound or thermal insulation, such as polystyrene. It was a true gamble that, in a short period of time, managed to revolutionize the very concept of seating, creating a clear break with the past of seat design. Colorful, extremely lightweight, and without a structure (I recall that it was the first armchair without a fixed structure), it quickly became the emblem of the young. They loved it because with this armchair, one could simply let go and its shapes allowed for relaxing in freedom.

The three designers stated that their goal was to create a flexible seat that '*could adapt, much like the snow where one throws oneself and leaves the shape of one's body.'* Zanotta, who had already embraced numerous nonconformist projects, accepted the proposal to put it into production.

When it was first introduced to the American market, it was called 'Bean Bag,' and subsequently, any product containing similar padding took its name from the 'bean bag'—the seat of the new generations, the fans of psychedelic and informal music, outside of any predefined posture, portable and friendly, in the spirit of the 1960s.

Thus was born the most revolutionary armchair, absolutely soft and nonconformist, that one could imagine. In an interview with a newspaper in January 1969, the three young architects stated that they drew inspiration for their project from sacks in which farmers would store chestnuts once harvested. During a moment of rest while they were still students looking for odd jobs, they sat on these sacks and found them extremely comfortable.

Immediately put into production by Zanotta, it conquered the public and the shop windows of the whole world in a very short time.

Regarding the meeting with Zanotta, Gatti stated in an interview with the online magazine Zanotta Happenings in 2008:

*'First of all, we say "the Sacco seat," not the armchair. Sacco has nothing to do with an armchair. Therefore, the first model of Sacco, assembled after several trials, was made of fairly sturdy transparent PVC, filled with polystyrene balls and with a handle for easy transport.*

*But I want to emphasize that for us, it was not a "pop" invention, but a targeted design of a rational object,*

*composed of two elongated hexagons for the upper and lower bases and sewn wedges that fit together.*
*We started cutting pieces of transparent plastic into "wedge" shapes, almost 2 meters high, and our mothers sewed them together so that we could have a complete idea. Then we went to a craftsman who did thermowelded plastic, the one used for document holders. He made us a first prototype that we called 'Moll you are,' meaning 'shaped by yourself.' Although it was a bit rough, we had it photographed and it didn't turn out bad. It was published in a magazine called 'Long Furniture Daily,' and it caught the attention of a purchasing manager from the department store 'Macy's,' who was fascinated by it. He immediately ordered 10,000 pieces. It was at that moment that we went to Zanotta, who immediately understood the potential of the seat and decided to put it into production.*
*The name 'Moll you are' that we had given to the prototype didn't satisfy us much, so we looked for another one that was more refined. We decided on 'Scrotum,' which means 'container' in Greek, but Zanotta felt it was too linked to the sexual sphere, so we settled on Sacco. It was a resounding, unforgettable success. It is the only seat that adapts to the person sitting on it, transforming each individual into the 'designer' of their own relaxation.'*[6]

It is from here that its success was born: from the combination of absolute flexibility with distinctive design, which quickly transformed it into a timeless icon. In 1970, it was awarded the Compasso d'Oro, a prestigious

6 Taken from an interview with Piero Gatti by Maria Ghianda in 2018

design award presented by ADI (Industrial Design Association). As mentioned before, in 1972, it was exhibited alongside other objects at the 'The New Italian Landscape' exhibition, garnering tremendous acclaim. But the biggest publicity for it did not come from MoMA or other exhibitions or museums, but from a hilarious scene in the film series featuring the character Fracchia (who later became Fantozzi), where an awkward Paolo Villaggio, invited by his boss to sit in front of him, asks timidly, *'On the armchair...?'* The boss replies, *'Yes, on the armchair!'* And here begins a real struggle (with punches) to sit on the armchair, which invariably keeps throwing him to the ground. This hilarious scene, widely broadcast on television, brought Sacco literally into the homes of many Italians, and at the time, it was better known as 'Fantozzi's armchair.

Paolo Villaggio portrays 'Fracchia the Human Beast.' 1981
(Property of Maura International Film)

**Table lamp "Eclisse"**
Vico Magistretti
ARTEMIDE 1965

The lamp is composed of 3 hemispheres: one at the base and
two others, one inside the other, which partially diffuse the
light. During those years, dimmers to change the intensity of
light did not exist, so it represented an absolute novelty.
Awarded the Compasso d'Oro in 1967, Eclisse is part of the
permanent collection of the MoMA in New York and the
Triennale di Milano."

# "It's truly an idea worthy of the 'Miserables'!"

**Intuition and creativity are crucial elements in the process of creating a design object. Intuition provides the initial inspiration, while creativity transforms that inspiration into something concrete and innovative.**

This object manages to perfectly combine the three main characteristics of design: form, functionality, and innovation, to the point of becoming perhaps the most famous Italian object in the world of design. This iconic and multi-award-winning lamp was created by Ludovico (Vico) Magistretti, a Milanese architect (from a family of three generations of artists), in the early 1960s. When Magistretti received the commission directly from Ernesto Gismondi, the founder of Artemide, to design a small bedside light, he was tasked with creating a lamp that could vary the intensity of the light beam to adjust it according to the needs of the moment. At that time, variable intensity lamps did not yet exist, essentially having only a simple on-off switch. The problem was not easily solved, and Magistretti himself said he had an unexpected intuition.

Magistretti recounted, *"It was 1963, and I was at Artemide in Piazza della Conciliazione in Milan, talking to Ernesto Gismondi, who said to me, '...Architect, everyone has beds, so why don't we make* *a bedside lamp that would be useful to many peo-ple?"* Magistretti listened attentively to his requests and returned to his studio to organize his thoughts. He took the M1 subway, which was fast and convenient, from Conciliazione to Palestro, just 6 stops away, a little over 15 minutes. Somewhere along the way, he had the right inspiration. Perhaps it was in the subway, aided by the dim light of the mezzanine, that he remembered a passage from Victor Hugo's novel "Les Misérables," describing Jean Valjean, the protagonist thief, escaping from the gendarmes in the darkness of the night. "...but the patrol resumed their march, leaving Valjean behind, who, amidst all that movement, saw nothing except the eclipse of the lantern."* In Magistretti's mind, he imagined a faint light in the distance, like a pulsating sphere, and perhaps at that precise moment, he had the intuition of a variable intensity lamp based on the concept of the blind lantern used by railway workers, where a light source is placed behind a door that opens and closes, modulating the light as desired. A hemisphere as a base, a hemisphere as a lampshade, and within it, another slightly smaller hemisphere inserted above the pivot to adjust the light: that could be the valid idea he was seeking. Magistretti continued to recount, *"I wanted to take a note so as not to forget, but I had nothing to write on, so I used the small subway ticket I had in my pocket. In just a few square centimeters, I managed to capture my intuition."* Once he arrived in the studio, he picked up the phone to call Gismondi and described it to him without even having a proper project or sketch in his hands.

Magistretti loved to say that if an idea was good and immediately understandable, it could be explained simply verbally, without rushing to start drawing; he liked to call it Concept Design. Then came the idea of adding the metaphor related to astronomy: by representing the Sun-Earth-Moon system, the three hemispheres simulate what happens during a lunar eclipse, where the Earth's shadow cone partially or totally covers the lunar surface. Just like with the moon, the inner cap of the lamp also rotates, thus covering the emitted light. In this way, the user can achieve a more or less diffused gradation. Today, it seems normal to us, but in the 1960s, it was pure innovation. Imagination, creativity, and solid design. Here is the perfect path.

In reality, it was supposed to be more or less like this,

the mythical reminder by Magistretti.

An ATM ticket from the 1960s with a handwritten note.

Often, patents for certain objects are not based on the complete object itself but on specific components present. In the case of the Plia chair, it is an innovative hinge consisting of three metal discs that allow the chair to fold perfectly. Stackable when folded or unfolded, precise, functional, and with an elegant structure, Plia continues to be a success and is exhibited in some of the world's greatest Design museums.

# "Fortunately, people don't choose with their behinds."

**Emotions have a significant impact on our purchases, even if we're not always aware of it. Their presence is crucial in every decision-making process. Emotions help create preferences and influence the choice to purchase not just an ordinary object, but something truly "beautiful."**

The Plia chair represents the dawn of a new era of widespread acclaim for the use of plastic materials. Since its production began in 1967, over 7 million units of this folding chair model designed by Giancarlo Piretti and produced by Anonima Castelli, a company founded by Ettore Castelli in 1897 that initially focused on cabinetmaking, have been sold. Plia is a modern reinterpretation of the classic wooden folding chair, with a body made of mirror-polished aluminum and a transparent plastic backrest and seat.

The folding mechanism was considered a true innovation in those years, revolutionizing the design. The story of the birth of the Plia chair is quite fascinating. After several months of work, Piretti decided to give up on the project of a new folding seat. The reason for his decision lay in the suboptimal working environment, as everyone at Anonima Castelli was accustomed to working with wood rather than plastic. To make him feel more comfortable, Mr. Castelli Jr. gave him the keys to a small, well-equipped workshop where he could go whenever he needed to conduct his own experiments.

The study began with the flat joint, and the aluminum underwent a special process that required the addition of a core. *"In a way, you always have to put your soul into it, especially when you're creating a folding chair, meant to be used when needed and not as a well-placed object in a room,"* said Piretti.

The tubes had to be thin to give the final product the right lightness, ensuring that it did not appear heavy in any way. To achieve greater lightness, the backrest and seat had to be transparent. Finding the right transparent material was not easy. During those years, ABS was in vogue, but it was quickly discarded due to its rapid opacification. Then, one day, Piretti recalled a visit he had made to Bayer in Germany some time earlier, where they were studying a transparent material called Cellidor, made with 45% cellulose. It was a material used in the production of sunglasses lenses but could also be well-suited for a chair, considering subsequent improvements that made it stronger.

The initial comfort tests for Plia received negative feedback. A test was conducted in England where blindfolded individuals were invited to sit on the chair, and Plia ranked fourth. However, shortly after, another test was carried out in which the same unblindfolded individuals were asked to choose the chair they liked the most, and Plia came in first.

*"Fortunately, people choose with their eyes and not with their behinds!"* Piretti remarked.

He continued, *"During those years, everyone loved Plia, an emergency chair, beautiful and fashionable. Just think, its presentation at the Salone del Mobile was a resounding success.*

*On the first day, people visited the Castelli booth and left with the chair under their arm.*

*From the second day onwards, they were chained to it with a chain...*

*In 1972, Plia became part of Emilio Ambasz's exhibition at MoMA. It was everywhere, in films, in advertisements.*

*The reason was simple: it was beautiful, inexpensive, and practical. For all these reasons, over 1000 chairs were produced every day.*

*All sorts of things happened around Plia; they even photographed a girl sitting on it, but the strange thing was that in one of the shots, the girl was almost naked, and they also took a shot from underneath where her buttocks were visible..."*

**Chair "Panton"**
Verner Panton
VITRA 1967

The Panton Chair, also known as the Pantheon Chair, embodies the designer's dream of creating a chair made from a single piece. Made entirely of plastic and without legs, the Panton Chair stands out for its bold and innovative design. It can be said that its main purpose is not utility, but rather to be a narrative object, beautiful and capable of going beyond the common use of many objects.

# "This plastic is terrible, it breaks like a biscuit!"

**A brilliant idea is just the beginning of a successful product. Especially when it is innovative, it brings significant challenges that require enlightened investors, competent technicians, and sometimes a lot, lot of time.**

The 1960s has always been referred to as the era of Space Age, as the race between nations to reach space was in full swing. The United States and Russia were in constant competition, and the first moon landing took place in 1969.

The public's enthusiasm for everything futuristic gave rise to a style called *Space Age*, where the protagonists were furniture in the shape of pods followed by uniquely shaped capsules.

Danish designer Verner Panton had been working on the idea of a one-piece plastic chair for over a decade. He drew inspiration from Gerrit Rietveld's *ZigZag* chair from 1932 and the cantilever chair *Sitzgeiststuhl* (The Chair of the Sitting Spirit) from 1927 by the brothers Heinz and Bodo Rasch.

Panton's dream began in the 1950s when he observed a stack of buckets and thought it would be fantastic to recreate the same concept with a chair designed as a single piece.

In 1956, he managed to create the S-Chair, a well-designed chair where the "S" shape of the seat was comfortable and followed the contours of the person sitting on it.

In 1960, Panton created a somewhat rudimentary prototype in plaster and then in fiberglass because the plastic materials that could achieve the desired shape did not yet exist. However, he faced technical production difficulties that he couldn't overcome on his own. He realized he needed help and embarked on a journey with his wife and the prototype in search of a manufacturer who believed in his idea. Many tried but declined his proposal, deeming it too challenging to manufacture.

After facing numerous rejections, Panton decided to return home and temporarily set aside the challenging project, focusing on other things.

After five long years, Willi Fehlbaum, the founder of Vitra (a Swiss furniture manufacturer and importer of Herman Miller, an American furniture company), visited Panton's workshop. He saw the prototype of the chair and asked why it wasn't in production.

Panton replied, *"Around 15 to 20 manufacturers have already tried, but for one reason or another, they all refused to manufacture it."*

The seat was quite unstable, and an American designer even said that the unique shape made it completely unsuitable for seating. However, Fehlbaum was so fascinated that he discussed the problem with the production's technical manager, Manfred Diebold, who found a proper approach to tackle the issue.

Working closely with Fehlbaum and Diebold, Panton conceived a model that could be cold-molded using polyester reinforced with fiberglass. This was the first time a chair was realized as a single piece, without legs, and yet stable.

However, this model was not entirely lightweight and required several finishing steps. Over the years, improvements were made to adapt it to industrial production by using thermoplastic polystyrene, resulting in a significant reduction in cost.

In 1968, Vitra started production using "Luran-S," a high-strength foam compound manufactured by Basf in Leverkusen, Germany. But after a few years, in 1979, the inevitable happened—the plastic yellowed over time and, most importantly, crumbled like a biscuit.

The problem was severe, and production was halted for fifteen years. It was only towards the late 1990s that the appropriate plastic compound was identified: expanded polyurethane, a material widely used in the 1980s for producing car dashboards.

In essence, between the conception and production, forty long years passed, and throughout this period, Fehlbaum and Panton never stopped believing.

It was an unstoppable success of a comfortable chair, thanks to its sinuous design that seemed to follow the body's lines.

During those years of studying the seat, there were moments of great despair when Verner would look despondently at his prototype, unsure of what to do. Legend has it that it was his wife who convinced him to show the chair to manufacturers. Tired of seeing him with a disheartened look, she said, *"Vernon, just look at it! It's beautiful. Show it to someone, and surely you'll find someone who wants to produce it. Either you go for it, or I'll ask for a divorce."*

By 1999, the chair was perfect, and Panton had also found the exact shade of red he had been seeking. He was finished. (In a way, his wife was finished too and asked for a divorce...) With its youthful and dynamic shape, and its powerful color, it became a symbol of the Pop Art movement.

Panton's work has always been characterized by a courageous use of color. In an interview, he stated, *"Most people go through life living in a dull gray conformity (think of today's cars...), with a deadly fear of using colors. The purpose of my work is to provoke people to use their imagination and make the surrounding environment more exciting."*

When his work was featured in the Danish design magazine Mobilia in 1967, it caused a sensation. In 1970, it was even included in the British fashion magazine Nova with a sequence of photos illustrating "How to Undress in Front of Your Husband."

Perhaps the most famous appearance of the chair occurred in January 1995 when it was featured on the cover of British Vogue.

The photograph by Nick Knight also included a completely nude girl.

As people looked at the photo, they noticed that besides Kate, there was also Verner's chair...? It's a question that still arouses a lot of curiosity today!

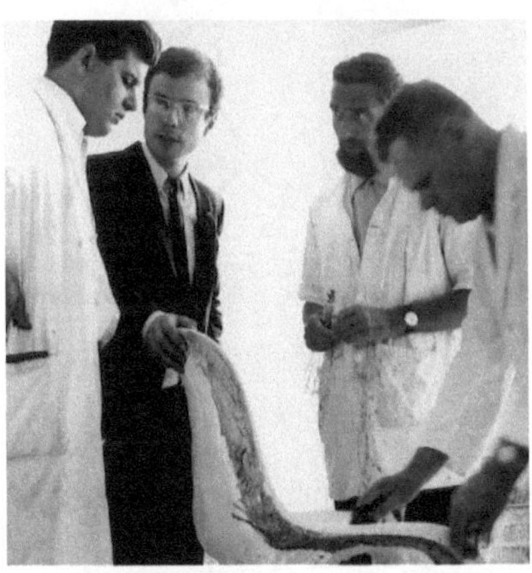

(Manfred Diebold -Willi Fehlbaum -Verner Panton
with a fiberglass prototype)

# Table Lamp "Anglepoise 1227"
## George Carwardine
### HERBERT TERRY AND SON 1931

This is the first lamp with spring arms that allow you to lock the direction of the light wherever you prefer. In fact, the purpose of the springs is not to pull or push as it may seem obvious, but only to stop at a certain point in accordance with the other three.

# "A lamp with car suspensions?"

**All the objects that surround us, even if they appear completely "modern," have roots in the past. They are objects that have influenced what came after, becoming archetypes of the past.**

How many of you have come across a lamp characterized by long arms and springs? This type of lamp has a well-defined history, to the point that those produced today can be considered faithful replicas of the first table lamp created using this methodology: the Anglepoise, the first balanced-arm table lamp in history.

It all started with an idea from British engineer George Carwardine, who resigned from his job designing car suspensions to pursue an idea that had been brewing in his mind for some time.

His goal was to create mechanical systems with a permanent tension character, allowing them to remain in perfect balance thanks to the structure of springs and levers.

In 1931, the first application of this project came to life in a table lamp. Thanks to a system of four springs and an articulated arm, the lamp could be directed wherever desired.

For the time, this invention represented a significant step forward, although initially its use was primarily in the industrial and military sectors.

The revolution was not only inherent in its ingenious structure but also in the fact that it could still be used in the absence of electricity by utilizing the low voltage of the built-in battery. Its success was also determined by its top-notch components, such as aluminum, steel, and Bakelite (the first true plastic in history), once again testifying to its extraordinary construction quality.

Its quality was further confirmed by the discovery of a British aircraft, a Vickers Wellington bomber, which had been submerged in Loch Ness for over 40 years following an emergency landing. Recovered in 1985, it was brought to the hangar for restoration. During an inspection of the aircraft's interior, an Anglepoise lamp was found still mounted on the cartographer's table.

These lamps had been commissioned to illuminate the aircraft's interior during navigation so that cartographers could read maps. After being properly cleaned of decades' worth of mud and dirt and having its battery replaced, the lamp was turned on for the first time, much to the amazement of those present.

This incident is undoubtedly a great testament to a well-designed project, where there is a careful balance of various factors: technique, functionality, innovation, and the quality of the materials used.

Before closing this story, I want to unveil the story of another lamp whose history intertwines with that of the Anglepoise.

The L1 lamp, very similar to the Anglepoise, was created by Norwegian engineer Jacob Jacobsen, the same person who founded Luxo in 1934, a company that traded sewing machines.

In 1937, a simple coincidence managed to change his story: the sewing machine supplier included two Anglepoise lamps along with the delivery, which were perfect for being mounted near the sewing machine to provide more light on the work surface. When Jacobsen opened the crates containing the machinery, he was struck by those two innovative lamps, understood their potential, studied them, and made modifications that earned him an invention patent (US Pat N. 2787434).

This allowed him to sell the "L1" lamps under his Luxo brand.

Sometimes you may come across this lamp called "Naskaloris." The reason is that a few years later, Jacobsen, perhaps to differentiate himself from Luxo (Textile Machinery), founded Naskaloris, his new company producing "balanced quadrilateral" lamps. Over the years, these lamps spread to the technical studios of architects, engineers, and workshops near machinery, becoming a global success.

In 1997, Naskaloris was acquired by Fontana Arte, which still produces it today under the name "Naska."

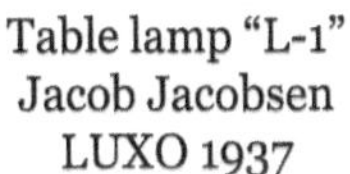

Table lamp "L-1"
Jacob Jacobsen
LUXO 1937

Dieter Rams designed this handheld calculator for Braun in 1981, which was a breakthrough compared to all the other calculators available on the market. Instead of rectangular buttons and square shapes, it featured a soft and rounded structure with colored circular buttons.

# "If the Apple guy copied me, I am honored."

**Is there a precise formula or specific rules to follow accurately in order to design a perfect object? Today, to some extent, yes, but in the past, no.**

Dieter Rams was a student at the Hochschule für Gestaltung, the "School of Design," in Ulm, Germany. In the 1960s, he was hired by Braun, where he designed numerous products that were seemingly simple. He explained his design philosophy with the expression *"Less but better"*. The most important characteristics of the objects he designed were elegance, immediacy, ease of use, and minimal design.

Dcades later, Jonathan Ive, the chief designer at Apple, drew inspiration from several of Dieter Rams' projects to the extent that many of his own designs appeared to be copies. If you're curious and want to see for yourself, simply search for *"Braun calculator and iPhone" on Google, as this is where you'll find the fine line between "quotation" and "copy."*

Upon closer inspection, it's easy to notice many similarities between the Braun ET 66 calculator and the iPhone's calculator. This is because Steve Jobs himself, along with his chief designer Jonathan Ive, held a deep admiration for Dieter's philosophy and his simple and innovative creations. Their inspiration extended beyond just the calculator and encompassed numerous iconic Apple products of that era. Dieter Rams is renowned in the world of design because the objects he created have become part of millions of people's lives. Just think of the electric toothbrush, the razor, the calculator, the stereo, or the alarm clock from Braun. These products changed the design landscape because they were not only simple but also beautiful. It was during those years that the unmistakable Apple or Braun styles were created. Rams had a clear idea about design, advocating for a stripped-down approach devoid of unnecessary elements. The product should not be burdened by what it doesn't need.

Rams was also one of the first to test the systemic design approach, conceptualizing objects from their core, where components were connected to their subsequent use. This approach, which he called "good design," anticipated contemporary criticisms regarding sustainability and planned obsolescence, the latter referring to a product's lifecycle intentionally limited to a specific timeframe.

With the sole objective of answering the question, *"Is my design good design?"* Rams formulated his ten key principles of good design, which established guidelines supporting simplicity, honesty, and moderation in countless design objects that still surround us today.

Steve Jobs and Jonathan Ive understood this well: for successful public reception, good design should contain as little design as possible, and their inspiration from Dieter Rams was immediate.

During an interview, Rams shared an anecdote about the "Apple" matter. At an event, he saw French designer Philippe Starck walking towards him, saying, *"Apple has copied you!"* Surprised by this statement and the manner in which it was delivered, Rams replied to Starck, quoting Charles Caleb Colton, *"Imitation is the sincerest form of flattery. If Ive was inspired by my work, I can only be honored."*
Clearer than this...

The Braun calculator compared to the iPhone's.

The N.14, the first mass-produced chair in history. Made from 18 pieces of steam-bent wood, assembled without glue and with only 10 screws. The back legs and backrest are a single long beech rod. The seat is woven with a dense pattern using *"Vienna straw"*.

# "Give me 36 eggs or a liter and a half of wine... or the chair!"

**Staying up to date with materials and new production technologies is a fundamental requirement for a designer, but sometimes luck can also play a role.**

The Number 14, the first chair in history to be mass-produced, tells the story of technological innovation in an exceptional way. I bet that each one of you has come across it at some point in your life, whether in a bar, at your grandparents' house, in a trendy café, bistros, or even on the internet. The Thonet Number 14 is the first example of Industrial Design, or rather the first piece of furniture with a large-scale serial production behind it. It represents a great classic among chairs and is one of the most famous in history, thanks to its innovative production characteristics.

Our journey into history takes us back to the early 19th century, specifically to Boppard, a small town in Prussia where the cabinetmaker Michael Thonet lived with his large family.

For some time, Thonet had been tirelessly experimenting with bending wooden bars forcefully, aiming to surpass the traditional technique that involved joining and sanding various pieces of wood or overlaying laminates, which tended to come apart over time. *Bend or break* became somewhat of his motto.

For years, he brought different branches of wood with varying diameters into his workshop. He completely immersed them in glue and then bent them, hoping that they would stiffen in the desired position during the drying process. The final result was never what he desired; the branches would bend to some extent, but it was quite challenging to force them into a precise shape.

Furthermore, the curves obtained were irregular and unsatisfactory to his requirements.

The attempts continued until one day something curious happened. He accidentally left some strips of wood outside his workshop door, and it rained heavily during the night. In the morning, as they were all wet, he placed them near the stove to dry. Unbeknownst to him, one of these small-diameter strips bent on its own. It was only two days later that he noticed the strip retained the desired curve. He was thrilled with excitement, repeated the experiment, and observed that damp strips of wood, when bent to assume a curvature, would maintain it if they dried slowly in front of a heat source.

Thanks to this fortunate discovery, he soon succeeded in replicating the desired effect on a serial scale. The wood was soaked for several days, and once drained of water, it was shaped into sinuous forms and clamped at the ends using irons and clamps until it dried slowly and completely in front of the fireplace. When the strips of wood were released, they maintained the sought-after curve.

It was 1830, and he had stumbled upon one of the most important techniques in wood processing: steam bending. It was simply fantastic.

However, this was just the beginning, as it took him some more time to perfect the technique. Instead of water, he started using steam at 104°C for about six hours, and the drying process occurred in a special oven where the wood remained for two days, effectively replacing the workshop's fireplace. The trials, drawings, and related prototypes continued. Beechwood served as the structure, while Vienna straw was used for the seat.

Many models came out of that workshop until the perfect design was achieved.

The creation of the perfect model occurred a few years later when the cabinetmaker was commissioned to create elegant chairs for Café Daum, a modern bar in Vienna awaiting its grand opening.

Thonet was ahead of his time and understood before anyone else that the secret to selling the chair lay in shipping it disassembled and having the user assemble it (just as Ikea does today). He made various attempts, and on the 14th try (hence the name given to the chair), he managed to create one composed of only six pieces, held together with ten screws. For the very first time, the backrest formed a single piece with the rear legs in one elegant and finely turned curve.

Finally, and no small feat, he was able to fit 36 disassembled chairs into a one-cubic-meter crate to be reassembled in the store and sold to the end user.

This method ensured significant cost savings. The Number 14 possessed the following characteristics: robustness, simplicity, and affordability. It cost three florins (equivalent to three dozen eggs or one and a half liters of wine). In those years, a worker's monthly wage was about 40 florins.

In 1860, production began, and its structure was extremely lightweight and resistant. As a testament to its durability, during the 1867 Expo, the chair was even dropped from the Eiffel Tower, falling a distance of 57 meters. To everyone's surprise, it remained intact, generating great interest. The key feature of this chair was its indestructibility. Once sold, if kept dry, it would never return.

After 10 years, that small workshop became the world's largest furniture factory. It has been estimated that over 50 million units were sold from its inception until 1930. It remained an unchanged success over the years and continues to be appreciated and copied worldwide as the finest curved wood chair that exists.

Its essential design became its strength, appealing to everyone, including nobles, artists, and politicians. It was the preferred chair of Tolstoy, Renoir, Brahms, Lenin, Marilyn Monroe, and Liza Minnelli... A chair that has also been honored in the world of painting throughout the ages. An icon capable of representing a unique and incomparable beauty, lasting forever.

Gebrüder Thonet, founded in 1854 in Vienna by
Michael Thonet and his five sons, was a significant

Wood bending process at the Thonet factory

**Sofa "Marylin"(Bocca)**
Franco e Nanà Audrito
GUFRAM 1970

The Marilyn chair, with its provocative and oversized design, soon became somewhat of a mascot and symbol of Pop Art. The seat and backrest of Marilyn are made of soft foam, while the upholstery is in the unmistakable red elasticized fabric by Gufram. Today, one can admire one of the original Marilyn chairs at the Triennale Design Museum in Milan.

# "Lawyer, don't be smart and bring the letter from Dalí…"

**Celebrities, with their personalities, have always been a source of inspiration. They are men and women who have had the courage to undertake great projects and change the style of the era they lived in. Many of these projects have become part of history, and we still refer to them as icons today.**

In the mid-1960s, some young designers, in opposition to rationalism, began creating objects that were completely outside the traditional frameworks, still known today for their irony and eccentricity. While these objects served a purpose, they also conveyed character and passion. Some designers questioned why an object should only adhere to principles of convenience when it had the potential to astound in a sensational way.

This is likely why designers are often referred to as "eccentric artists." The Marilyn sofa fits perfectly into this context because it symbolizes a period where appearance prevailed over essence. It was during the 1960s that the concept of stereotypical and glossy beauty emerged, promoted by many fashion magazines.

What appeared was more important than thought or quality, to the extent that the Marilyn sofa fully embodies this line of thought, becoming a sort of testament to it. Now that I've explained what it represented, I believe it's important to understand how Marilyn came to be.

Franco Audrito, the founder of Studio65, tells the story: *"It was 1970 when Marilyn Garosci, owner of a chain of fitness centers in Milan, asked me to design a wellness center for her, the Contourella in Milan.*

*We designed everything, from the flooring to the walls, the seating, even the office desk and lamps, but we couldn't find anything suitable for the entrance of this beauty temple. Then we remembered Salvador Dalí's painting, 'The Portrait of Mae West' (a singer from the '30s considered a sex symbol of the time). The face of the diva was represented by objects placed in an imaginary room, where the mouth was depicted by a sinuous sofa.*

*That was the inspiration we needed for the entrance.*

*We created a sofa in the shape of a mouth and had it produced by Gufram, a company that had made a name for itself in those years for manufacturing soft and colorful foam armchairs and sofas.*

*While the sofa was still at Gufram's headquarters, it caught the attention of a journalist from Casa Vogue magazine, who couldn't resist taking a photo and publishing it. Shortly after, the sofa appeared for the first time in an issue of the American magazine Life, with the young model Marisa Berenson sitting provocatively, and that shot sealed its worldwide success in the market.*

*That's when Dalí found out about it and wrote us a letter asking for explanations. We promptly apologized for the misunderstanding and made sure to provide the correct information. That was the end of it, and Dalí was a true gentleman. We named the sofa Marilyn (and not Bocca) in honor of the full lips of the ultimate Hollywood pop diva (but also as a tribute to our client's name, Marilyn Garosci, who was also blonde with fiery red lips). Then someone started calling it 'Bocca,' and we were fine with that too.*
*Our lawyer insisted on keeping Dalí's letter for himself instead of accepting payment for his fees.*
*However, it seems that it has been lost today, alas."*

Franco Audrito and Salvador Dalí in front of the
original sofa created by the painter.

**Armchair "Joe"**
De Pas, D'Urbino, Lomazzi
POLTRONOVA 1971

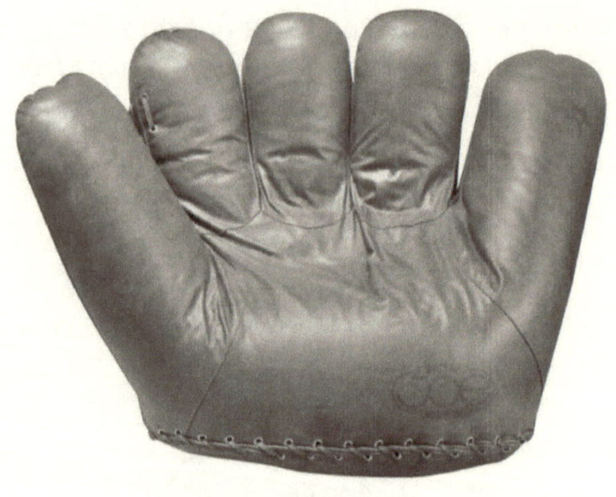

*Joe is an "important" armchair with XXL dimensions that faithfully reproduces a baseball glove in every aspect. It features leather upholstery, cords, stitching, laces, and eyelets just like a real baseball glove. Hidden underneath the base are small invisible wheels for easy mobility.*

# "Let's do it, out of scale, out of place, out of our minds."

**The ability of a designer to uniquely observe their surroundings is essential for creating both astonishing and functional objects. The designer must be capable of capturing the most singular and unusual aspects of reality, transforming them into original and unconventional solutions.**

An enormous baseball glove stands out in the middle of the room like a big hand ready to receive something (or someone). This seat represents a total deviation from all past patterns, it's pure fun, pure humor, it's Pop Art invading the house and making it unique.

It is called Joe in honor of the super Italian-American baseball champion Joe DiMaggio. The creators are a trio that has permanently marked the history of world design. Their group takes its name from the initials of their surnames: DDL, Jonathan De Pas, Donato D'Urbino, and Paolo Lomazzi.

How did they come up with such a groundbreaking project? Intuition, creativity, and a great understanding of the subject matter from a technical, stylistic, and historical perspective like no other.

How does a project like this start?

Imagine an evening of design brainstorming at home; one of the three takes a baseball and a glove

displayed prominently on a shelf in the living room. Someone says, *'Nice, whose glove is this?'*
*'Put down my Joe DiMaggio glove... just like it.'*
They pound their fist into the glove.
*'I've always liked the sound the ball makes when the catcher catches it from the pitcher... "PAACCC"... yeah, a nice sharp sound it makes, perfect for a ball.'*
*'If it were for the seat, it would make a "PSSCIIIT" sound, a soft sound like a sofa cushion.'*
*'A cushion? Wait a minute, I've got an idea... do you know Claes Oldenburg's [7] oversized sculptures? He's that sculptor known for his giant installations made of everyday objects.'*
*'Yes, I know, Charles Eames did something similar too. In 1956, he designed his famous Lounge Chair and Ottoman, describing it as 'giving a warm appearance like a first baseman's glove in baseball.'*
*'And let's make it like that... a leather baseball glove.' 'Yes, exactly... and what if the glove were enormous... a giant sofa? Let's make it 'Zoom,' XXL, out of place, out of scale, out of the ordinary, out of everything.' '*
*I like this healthy madness you have right now, well done.'*
*'A bit like Audrito's "Bocca" sofa?'*
*'Yes, exactly.'*
*'Come on, who would ever put a glove/sofa in their living room?' 'Wanna bet...?'*
The rest is history. The DDL trio enjoy creating products that I would call astonishing, yet still functional. It is precisely in furniture and furnishing acces-

---

[7] Claes Oldenburg is the author of the sculpture "Needle, Thread, and Knot" located in Cadorna Square in Milan.

sories that their revolutionary spirit shines the most. With a bold shift in scale, they transformed the baseball glove into a welcoming place to sit. An object defined as iconic, capable of telling the extraordinary abilities of Italian design during that period. A creativity that turns a common object into something truly artistic. In this era, we invent new ways of sitting, but don't be fooled by Joe's playful appearance because anyone who sits on it is fascinated by its comfort. Even its design was a challenging process from the beginning. Experimenting with different materials, they went from clay to plaster until they obtained a matrix to insert the polyurethane.

Paolo Lomazzi explains.

*'We worked a lot on the model: it was put on a pedestal, the same ones used for sculptures, then we placed jute bags on top because the clay was wet, and finally, we sat on it until we found the right shapes,'*
The audacity of the project is also demonstrated by the advertising campaign conceived by Poltronova.

*'At the time of Joe's debut, Sergio Cammilli, the founder of Poltronova, was afraid of the rights related to the name Joe (DiMaggio).*

*That's how, thanks to Paolo Lecci's intervention, the slogan 'JOE... di Maggio, Giugno, Luglio...' was created."* [8] A clever and winning advertising strategy. A trick that uses the names of months to confuse matters, but in the collective imagination, Joe will always remain the American baseball superstar and Marilyn Monroe's husband.

---

[8] Taken from an article in Elle Decor by Rosario Spagno-

*The Ericofon was created to be a practical and affordable telephone, typical characteristics of Scandinavian design, especially during those years. Its unique design, made in a single piece and with vibrant colors, contributed to its success at the time and continues to attract collectors worldwide. It is easy to find on the second-hand market due to the large number of units sold.*

# "Nurse, could you pass me the cobra?I can't reach it."

**Sometimes there are objects that maintain the same form for years, as if there were no other possibilities. But one day, a designer manages to completely break the mold and conceive a completely different shape, so incredible that it astonishes everyone.**

In some cases, the characteristics of the ideal design, as we have already mentioned, summarized in terms of form, aesthetics, and functionality, converge in a single object. This is the case of the Ericofon, an object that represents a turning point in telephone design.

Phone manufacturers around the world have always dreamed of creating a unique object. It is worth noting that originally, the Ericofon was designed for the professional market.

Regarding its name, the Swedes were the first to nickname it the "*Cobra*" phone, due to its shape resembling the snake of the same name. In truth, its distinctive shape was inspired by its initial target audience, namely hospitals.

In a hospital setting, using a phone with a separate handset and body while being confined to bed was a nightmare.

This led to the idea of creating a phone with a single body, a compact and practical form for everyone.

In 1939, Hugo Blomberg, the technical director of *Ericsson*, launched a competition asking participants to design a phone with a single body. The competition was won by Ralph Lysell, a highly creative designer who managed to convince everyone with his innovative presentation of renderings and clay models. Two years later, the project was at its peak, and Lysell quickly presented several sketches and various model proposals when the project was unexpectedly put on hold for eight years.

Only in 1949 did *Ericsson* pick up the project again, but in the meantime, Lysell had left *Ericsson* and was replaced by Gösta Thames, who created additional renderings and models.

In an interview given in the 2000s, Gösta Thames stated that industrial design had always been a point of great interest for him when he was a student, which is why he was chosen for the phone project due to a self-speaking phone he had designed. The exact combination of various design elements made the phone an attractive object.

Gösta was tasked with overseeing the development project, a job that would require several years and encompass various aspects. It took some time to incorporate the various components into the phone, but Thames was adamant about one thing: the *Ericofon* should not require a wall-mounted box to function; it had to be a single piece.

Over time, Thames, along with his colleagues, managed to reduce the size of the various components, including the transformer, so that they could all fit inside the phone's body.

Despite the promising start, an issue was immediately encountered: *Acrylite*, the material invented by Otto Rhom in 1936, was fragile, prone to scratching, and yellowed over time.

The solution came two years later with the invention of ABS, a glossy, highly durable, and colored plastic.

*"My starting point in choosing a shape has always been that the phone should be easy to hold. It should be light and comfortable in the hand. You should be able to feel how to hold it near your ear even in the dark."*

Through numerous improvements and ergonomic tests with Ericsson modelers, the one-piece phone eventually reached its final form.

Its unique design, user-friendly interface, luxurious colors, and high-quality finish completely broke away from the heavy black bakelite phones of the time.

With its modern appearance, 18 different shades (it was never made in black because it was considered too gloomy), and advertising campaigns in glossy magazines, it remained at the peak of success for nearly thirty years, selling over two million units.

*"Cobra"* was also the first Swedish phone to have a dedicated name rather than just a number. This particularity made a difference; the "Cobra" was perceived by people as a product, not just a simple extension of the phone's function.

In truth, Ericofon was not the original name used by *Ericsson*. Gösta Thames said in an interview, *"The people working on the project called it Erifon, com-*

*bining the first three letters of the company's name with the Greek word for sound. But when we tried to register the name, we found out that it was already being used for a fireproof fabric product. So, we had to find another name. The result was 'EriCOfon'; we simply added 'CO' in the middle as an abbreviation for 'Company'."*

The real success came when it was introduced to the American market by North Electric.

Like all phones of the time, the Ericofon had the classic rotary dial and a mechanical bell ringer. With the advent of the first miniaturized transistors in the late 1960s, the first model with a tweeter (chirping) ringtone was developed, replacing the metal bell and featuring touch-tone buttons for dialing. However, a problem arose: since the delicate hook/button (seen in the photo at the beginning) that turned the phone on and off was complex and fragile, slamming the phone down heavily would cause the expensive and hard-to-find combiner to break.

In 1972, North Electric ceased production and sold its remaining stock to Ceac, a company that produced them for a while and then limited itself to repairs. Numerous photographs and advertisements from those years can be found all over the internet and are definitely worth seeing. Today, this phone remains a fantastic example of how functionality, aesthetics, and technological innovation can naturally coexist in a single product.

As a testament to its enduring success, Wild and Wolf now produce a clone of the Ericofon called the Scandiphone, featuring a redesigned hook/button and a never-before-seen color that has become very trendy: black.

Advertisement of the Ericofon showcasing the qualities of the device used with one hand.

# Stool "SELLA"
### Achille e  Pier Giacomo Castiglioni
### ZANOTTA 1957

The *Sella* stool is composed of an actual bicycle saddle closed with the classic quick-release clamp and mounted on a steel tube that connects to a second tube in pink color (the color reminiscent of the winner's jersey in the Giro d'Italia). It is supported by a heavy semispherical cap that ensures its balance.

# "When I spend a long time on the phone, I get seasick."

**To properly evaluate an object that may seem too artistic or less functional, it is important to first ask yourself the reason why it was created in that specific way. Is it the result of a meticulous study by the designer or simply the product of a failed execution?**

The designer is often inspired by objects that may seem insignificant to most people, objects collected during travels or found by chance in markets or even in department stores, and then kept in display cases and drawers in the studio, only to be taken out and studied from time to time, serving as inspiration for new projects.

In Milan, at the Achille Castiglioni Foundation, you can visit the studio where Achille worked for over 60 years, first with his brother Pier Giacomo, and then, from 1968, on his own.

It's a unique kind of museum where you can walk through various rooms and observe projects, products, and prototypes accompanied by close collaborators or even Achille's daughter, Giovanna, who has been cataloging her father's lifelong work for years. It is in these rooms that, among other things, you can see some objects that Achille collected without an apparent reason, objects that would eventually serve a purpose. Objects that could possibly be transformed into something else.

But let's take a step back in time. It was in 1917 that the French artist Marcel Duchamp executed a "transformation of use," exhibiting a real ceramic urinal at an art show and calling it "Fountain." At that time, his purpose was to provoke a discussion about the role of the artist and art itself. The critics and the public distanced themselves from what was considered an indecent object that couldn't be regarded as a work of art simply because it was associated with bodily waste. However, Duchamp's gesture had repercussions on all subsequent art, breaking down the barriers between what could be defined as art and what was considered otherwise.

About forty years later, in Italy, the Castiglioni brothers utilized this "ready-made" or, as it was called, "Ready-Made" approach to propose common objects intended for different uses. For example, they transformed a tractor seat into a stool called "Mezzadro", a car headlight became a floor lamp called "Toio", and a bicycle saddle called "Sella" was turned into a seat, albeit a somewhat peculiar one.

The Castiglioni brothers took existing objects with a specific function and added the intuition that created refined design objects full of imagination and with a renewed function different from the primary one.

"Sella" was conceived to be a "dissuasive" telephone stool, using pre-existing industrial elements from an actual bicycle: the saddle with its seat post and quick release mechanism. At first glance, it may seem like an incongruous seat, but upon closer analysis, it reveals a well-thought-out design.

In the late 1950s, telephones were present in almost every household (and certainly not more than one), often mounted at head height in corridors, without considering the possibility of sitting down. Since making phone calls was expensive, parents (including mine) who paid the bills would remind their children that phone calls were meant for exchanging quick information, not for telling funny anecdotes to friends. However, since these words often fell on deaf ears, Achille, as a designer and keen observer of people, perhaps approached the problem differently.

He designed a stool that would subtly invite someone to sit down but, being rather wobbly (thus providing an uncomfortable or unstable seating experience in the long run), it would discourage long conversations.

Genius, isn't it?

This is how the intended purpose transforms what seemed like a less usable design project due to its precarious and unstable nature into a point of strength. That's why, in order to properly evaluate a design object, much like we do with a work of art, it is crucial to understand the motivations that led to that result.

# Sofa "Marshmallow"
### Irving Harper
### HERMAN MILLER 1956

With its shape resembling an open waffle iron, vibrant colors, and whimsical name, the Marshmallow sofa seemed to epitomize the emergence of the Pop Art era. The cushions, supported by a delicate steel structure, appeared to float in the air. When it first appeared on the market in 1956, the Marshmallow sofa's bold design, easy-to-clean surfaces, and almost invisible structure created a striking and evident contrast with the bulky, dust-collecting sofas with heavy upholstery that dominated many living rooms at that time.

# "George, do you want to taste a cushion?"

**A designer has an intimate and somewhat peculiar connection with their creations, a sort of material and mental relationship. It all starts when they come across an intriguing object that sparks their curiosity, and from there, an idea blossoms that has never been conceived by anyone else.**

George Nelson was an American designer widely regarded as one of the founders of the modernist design movement, which emerged in the 1920s and 1930s. During this period, innovation and aesthetics became harmoniously intertwined. As the head designer for *Herman Miller*, a furniture manufacturing company, Nelson was able to create futuristic furniture for the time. One of his talented collaborators was Irving Harper, a designer with great talent.

Irving, who lived to be 99 years old, recounted a curious anecdote about how the idea for a well-known sofa, commonly known as the *Marshmallow* sofa due to the unusual shape of its round and colorful cushions, came about during a weekend. In the spring of 1954, a rubber company from Long Island sent round pieces with a diameter of 12 inches to showcase their products. Upon opening the boxes and seeing those round cushions made of foam rubber,

Irving started contemplating their potential uses, generating various hypotheses. At one point, he had a brilliant idea and tried to get George's attention, who was working in the next room. Trying to entice him, Irving jokingly said, *"George, how about a Chamallow?* (A type of gummy candy produced by Haribo). *I assure you they are soft, fluffy, with a delicious and sweet flavor."* Nelson's response came swiftly, *"Before you eat them all, you need to devise a structure that can support those cushions."*
*"How about a round stool?"* Irving asked.
George immediately replied,
*"No, think bigger. Imagine 10 or 20 cushions, like marshmallows. I'll leave you to your thoughts. See you on Monday."*
Irving focused on the shapes of those large cushions, to the point that he designed a rather unusual sofa over that weekend, with an even more amusing name, Marshmallow.
This design object contributed to writing the history of worldwide design.
Just two years after the initial idea, production began. The only drawback was that the cushions were expensive, and their assembly took time. Despite being a good product, sales were low, with only 186 pieces sold. Failure seemed imminent with such poor sales, and production had to be halted.
Regarding this, Harper said, *"The sofa was meant to be a joke, a kind of game, because I had never done anything that seemed so particular. But it was well-received and immediately sent for prototyping. The only problem was that the plastics company that*

*supplied the cushions couldn't produce them in mass quantities as we wanted. This became a cost problem because they had to be practically handmade. So, instead of focusing on the sofa, you had to struggle to make those damn cushions for just one sofa. It was a nightmare, but there was no other way to do it at the time. It turned out to be more expensive than we anticipated, which was ridiculous, and that's why Herman Miller produced less than 200 pieces."*

It wasn't until the 1980s that new technology allowed for more efficient production optimization. When the sofa was reintroduced to the market, it became a resounding success.

A word about authorship (the sofa was always associated with George Nelson's creation): most people are unaware that in an interview, Harper said, *"George's attitude was that for the consumer world, the authorship of an object should always be attributed to the company, not the individual. I am grateful to George for what he did for me. While he was alive, I made no requests. But now that he's gone, every time the Marshmallow sofa is referred to as a 'design by George Nelson,' it bothers me a bit. I'm not trying to let the world know who made it, but if someone asks me who designed it, I'm perfectly happy to tell them."*

Personally, I can't help but think somewhat mischievously, *"Well, it's easy to say that after Nelson's death..."* However, there were numerous testimonies about George Nelson's work, thanks to Hilda Longinotti ("the woman on the Marshmallow sofa"), who confirmed the episode. Regarding the famous sofa, she revealed, *"The studio didn't have much money to pay a professional model. I was young, pretty, photogenic, and available. So, I became George's muse whenever they needed someone sitting on something."*

George Nelson e Irving Harper 1965
(Property of *House & Garden*)

*Hilda Longinotti, the "Woman on the Marshmallow
Sofa," in the mid-1950s.
(Property of Herman Miller)*

*Hilda Longinotti during an interview in 1999
(Property of Herman Miller)*

Electric lighter **"FireBird"**
Guido Venturini
ALESSI 1993

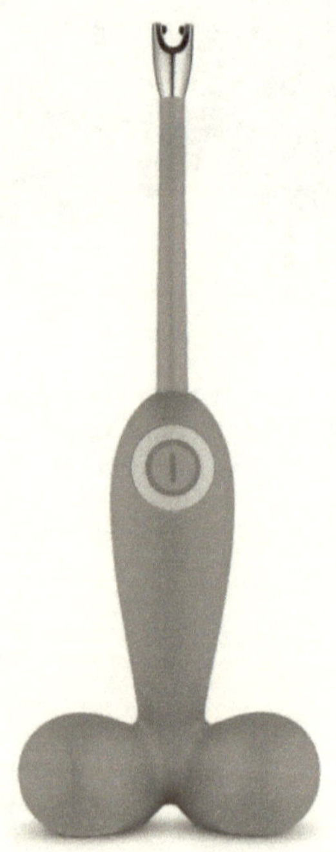

Reusable electric arc lighter made of colored thermoplastic resin, with an aluminum head that generates the electric spark. It operates without flammable liquids and does not produce a flame, but generates a small electric spark to ignite the gas.
"Firebird" is a kitsch object? You decide...

# "It ignites...?
# Passion, for sure."

**How to decipher an object with an unconventional shape? Perhaps within its bizarre lines, there lies a cultural message from the author, and it is up to us to unveil its subtle nuances. It is like trying to read between the lines of a stylistic enigma.**

Between an artist and a designer, there is a profound difference. The artist doesn't care about creating an object that pleases many people; their goal is to communicate their personal vision, not to please but to convey a message. The designer must consider multiple factors and cannot limit themselves to expressing their own vision through an object.

In this regard, I want to talk to you about Bolidism, a movement founded by Guido Venturini, born in 1957, an architect, designer, and painter. The movement was established in 1986 with the intention of communicating sensations through dynamic, slightly curved, and lightweight forms. Venturini initially collaborated with Stefano Giovannoni, and together they founded *King Kong Production*. Thanks to this partnership, they created some iconic objects, many of which are part of the Alessi brand, such as *Girotondo*, a basket made of mirror-effect steel, featuring

little figures holding hands all around its circumfe-
rence. The stylized little figure icon is linked to childhood memories and was a resounding success that
still endures today.
In many of their works, *King-Kong* expressed an interest in spontaneous objects, a series of charming
items to be placed in people's homes. The introduction of such different and surprising objects sparked
criticism from some snobbish individuals who di-
smissed them as banal. However, they were quickly
proven wrong by an enthusiastic wave of buyers ea-
ger to populate their kitchens with irreverent elves
and purely imaginative objects that seemed to come
straight out of Alice in Wonderland.
Their attempt was to bring design closer to popular
culture through the creation of simple objects. In
this regard, they hit the mark with *Girotondo*, surpassing even the expectations of marketing. In addition to *Girotondo*, there are many other creations,
including *Gino Zucchino* and *Firebird*.
*Gino Zucchino* represents the progenitor of the little
elves; it is a sugar dispenser whose forms strongly recall comics. It is an object capable of bringing a smile
and joy just by looking at it. *Gino Zucchino*, born in
1993, with its large eyes and wide smile, brings out
the child in everyone, offering moments of lighthear-
tedness during breakfast or coffee breaks.
On the other hand, *Firebirds* is a lighter labeled by
puritan minds as a kitsch object. This word comes
from German and indicates something of bad taste.

I believe that innovative design, even just in terms of form, cannot be considered kitsch. A kitsch object usually copies another recognizable object or artwork. If the lighter had resembled the shape of the Eiffel Tower, it could have been considered kitsch.

*Firebird*, on the other hand, is not kitsch because there is thought behind its creation, where the form somewhat surpasses its function. Venturini came from the world of comics, and perhaps his experience in that field led to the idea of creating a provocative plastic sculpture reminiscent of a phallus.

Firebird was born in a creative workshop in 1993, where they sought to understand the communicative dimension of objects, including their ability to amaze and emotionally connect with people. Over time, it has become a true icon, thanks to its delicate yet explicit allusion. It's worth noting that when it was discontinued, collectors actively sought it out, willing to pay significant sums just to have it in their collections.

One could describe it as a small, ironic, and irreverent sculpture to have in one's home, even using it as a lighter when needed. Although it may appear as a simple object today, we must consider that there is a lot of courage behind its creation, especially on the part of the manufacturer who released it onto the market without even knowing if it would be a success or a resounding flop.

The creative genesis of this particular object remains unknown. I like to imagine, with my imagination, its creator, Guido, in the evening while preparing dinner, searching unsuccessfully for a lighter, growing impatient and deciding to postpone the search after a quick pit stop in the bathroom. During this moment, perhaps fortuitously, a brilliant idea arises from a evidently very creative and provocative solution. They could create an object that would be different from all others, not necessarily hidden in pants but proudly displayed on a kitchen shelf, awaiting comments.

Allow my imagination to run free because I believe that such an object could only be born from a provocative and ultimately brilliant intuition…"

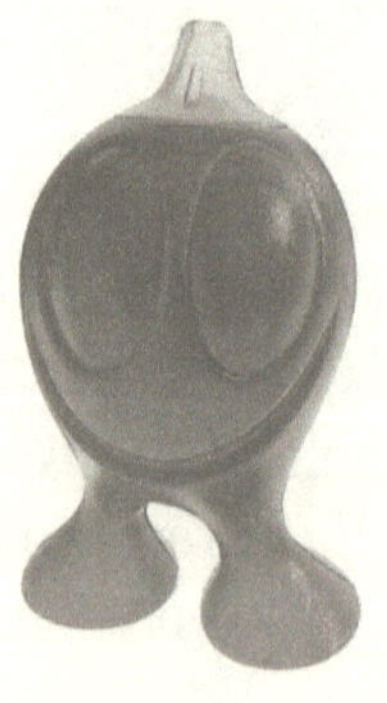

*Gino Zucchino*

*Girotondo*

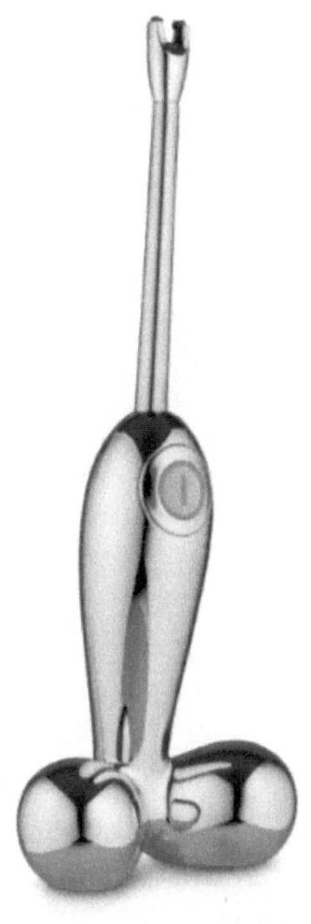

*Alessi gold Firebird*

The Tulip chairs are part of the collection designed by Eero Saarinen for Knoll in 1957. Tulip revolutionizes the rules of design by introducing the innovative concept of a single large central leg instead of the traditional four legs. Saarinen initially used fiberglass and later plastic to achieve this design.

# "To hell with these clean-shaven folks who can't hold their liquor."

**Indeed, it is truly remarkable to envision seemingly impossible objects, such as a chair without legs. However, we must acknowledge that complex needs require bold ideas and extraordinary solutions, coupled with absolute dedication to one's work.**

Eero Saarinen won his first design competition at the age of 12, thanks to an illustration he created with matches for a Swedish newspaper, earning him a prize of 30 crowns (approximately 80 euros). In fact, in '56, an article in *Time* magazine described him as a *'battery full of inexhaustible energy.'*

Eero, who later became an architect, grew up immersed in design, thanks in part to his father, a well-known architect, and his mother, a renowned sculptor and textile producer with immense talent. We can imagine this young boy playing under his father's drafting table or observing his mother's creativity. At the age of twelve, he was drawing nudes, and a few years later, at the age of twenty, he was designing furniture for his father's commissioned works at Cranbrook.

He went on to win numerous awards, to the point where he received a medal commemorating the number of accolades he had received. Upon completing his academic studies, as one might expect, he received high praise. Although his architectural works garnered numerous recognitions, to the extent that he graced the cover of *Time* magazine in '56, it is his furniture that is most celebrated in the twentieth century.

The Tulip Chair is one of these pieces. With its shape reminiscent of a flower or a stemmed glass, this chair was conceived primarily to alleviate the problem of clutter. In an interview, its creator revealed the intentions behind the project, stating, *'The 'underside' of chairs and tables in a typical apartment makes for an ugly, restless, and troubled world. I wanted to clear up the slum of legs. I wanted to make the chair all one thing again. We have chairs with four legs, with three legs, and with two legs, but no one has made one with just one leg, so we will.'*

Saarinen designed the Tulip Chair with a single leg that serves as both its form and function, creating a more harmonious environment without excessive congestion between chairs, tables, and stools. The chair embodies Saarinen's efforts to create a chair made of a single material, promoting the concept he held dear in design, *'one piece, one material.'*

At the time, it was not possible to produce a single-piece item with a single material, which caused some delays. The base was made through a metal casting process, as the technologies of the time did not allow plastic to have the necessary strength to support a seated person. The seat, made of fiberglass, appears to be composed of a single material, but it is actually supported by an aluminum stem with a fused plastic finish.

Saarinen eventually completed the entire collection in 1956, which included the chair, tables, and a stool. The patent design for the Tulip Chair was filed on June 7, 1960. This was his last creation, as he passed away a year later.

Even though he is no longer with us, he left behind a great legacy intertwined with his vision of the future, which has endured. The dedication he showed to his art is summed up in a legendary anecdote. Around eight in the morning on New Year's Eve, upon entering his studio and finding it empty apart from his assistant, he exclaimed in astonishment,

*Where the hell is everyone?'*

And the sole presence replied, '*...but it's the first of January, and it's a holiday...'*

Without much thought, he retorted, '*To hell with all these clean-shaven guys who can't hold their liquor!'*

*"Tolix,"* derived from the French word "Tole," means "sheet metal." In the case of Tolix, it refers to iron sheet metal coated with liquid zinc through a galvanic procedure. This treatment makes the metal resistant to rust. Tolix chairs are currently exhibited at the MOMA in New York and the Centre Pompidou in Paris. They are still being sold today.

# "Hey dad, do you have some extra zinc?"

**Mastery of different production techniques in all their nuances gives the designer extraordinary power. This expertise allows them to create cutting-edge objects that are in tune with the times, capable of stimulating commercialization and progress.**

Perhaps you are not familiar with the name of this chair, but you have most likely been in a place with an outdoor terrace and have probably sat on this chair before. Its name is the *Marais a chair,* or simply *Tolix*. It can be described as a simple, sturdy, and stackable seat. It is the invention of the creative genius, Xavier Pauchard, the son of a builder and zinc roofer from Burgundy, born in 1880. He had the pioneering idea of exploring the chemical process to protect sheet metal (used for roofs) from corrosion. Although the discovery dates back to 1742, it was not widely used in the following years. Xavier began experimenting with it in his garden after his daughter translated a technical treatise on the subject for him. This new technique was significant as it explained how to protect iron objects from oxidation by immersing them in molten zinc at 450°C. Xavier spent years perfecting his skills in working with iron and later steel until he could shape it into any desired form. At that point, he decided to establish a factory for producing household items in line with this newly discovered, or rather perfected, innovation.

Around the mid-1920s, he managed to create a highly useful product for outdoor seating, known as the "*Tolix Chaise*." Until then, public establishments used steam-bent wooden chairs (such as the Thonet chairs we encountered earlier) which were lightweight, stackable, and seemingly perfect. However, they had a significant problem: they were susceptible to water damage, and over the years, they had to be replaced at considerable expense for the venue owners. In a short time, Xavier Pauchard became the leading manufacturer of household items made from galvanized sheet metal in Burgundy. In 1927, he registered the *Tolix* trademark to accommodate his growing production of metal furniture, ranging from armchairs to stools.

*Tolix* was a true revolution. In addition to being beautiful, durable, and lightweight, it had another advantage—it was rust-resistant, thanks to the galvanization process his father had used on roofs. Soon, *Tolix* chairs conquered the interiors and exteriors of bars, terraces, parks, and numerous public spaces. The material used, galvanized sheet metal, possessed fire-resistant and hygienic properties, making it the perfect choice.

Stamped, bent, and then welded, with its curved backrest and its famous ornamental leaf, those amusing round front legs, hollow rear legs, and slightly flared shape to facilitate stacking, each chair required about a hundred operations, making each piece unique. It was truly a success. Within a short period, the chair could be found everywhere. In addition to the aforementioned qualities, it complemented any interior design due to its availability in 50 different colors.

It is impossible to get rid of a *Tolix* chair. The carefully crafted and painted galvanized metal is resistant to everything: time, weather, and even transportation. There are not many design icons that, no matter where they are placed, seem to be designed precisely for that space, but the A chair is one of them.

In 1952, Pauchard made a bet with a restaurant owner who challenged him, claiming that his chairs were too bulky and that he could never stack more than two of them. The following year, Xavier modified the structure of the seat and managed to create a particular geometry where 25 chairs of the "A" model fit perfectly into a cabinet slightly over 2 meters tall. The bet was won.

If you have such a cabinet at home, stack all the chairs inside, and now you only need a table for 25 friends. (The cabinet won't be enough...)"

# Table Lamp "KD27"
Joe Colombo
KARTELL 1961

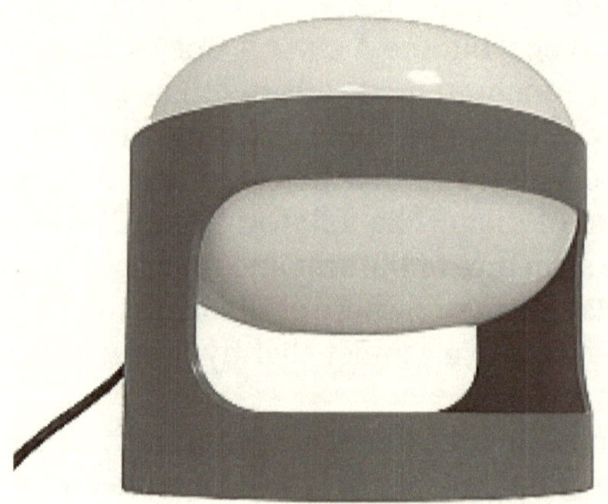

A hollow cylinder made of ABS resin holds a double circular shell that serves the purpose of shielding the incandescent light bulb. It is a table lamp that has made its mark in the history of Italian design and Kartell's production.

# "Nooo, don't cut it!! Gino is sensitive about it."

**Can we take an existing object and transform it into something completely new, with a completely different purpose from the original? Can we consider it as an example of design?**

The Castiglioni brothers, Achille and Giacomo, at a precise moment in history, amidst their countless projects, would take existing objects and reconceive them for another purpose. Around the mid-1950s, this way of thinking was called Ready-Made, which means 'Ready for use.' It was a thought that emerged during those years but fell within the realm of pure creativity. In this case, however, it wasn't about quoting or copying the object, but rather reworking it by a designer and an entrepreneur.

Joe Colombo, born Cesare Colombo, who was dubbed 'the prophet of design' in 2000, was undoubtedly one of the most brilliant designers in the world. He was an artist and designer from Milan, born in 1930, who tragically passed away in 1971 at the young age of 40, leaving behind a vast conceptual legacy for those who followed in his footsteps. Joe initially dabbled in various artistic projects, followed by an interest in avant-garde painting and sculpture, before delving into everyday objects. He discovered that Design, as he called it, was primarily about 'imagining the possible.' As early as the 1960s, he foresaw the transformations that technological development would bring to everyday life, and he created a series of truly incredible objects that remain remarkable both in form and substance to this day.

Much of what has been preserved is owed to his young assistant, Ignazia Favata, who diligently cataloged all of Colombo's materials over the years, making them accessible to everyone. Speaking of Joe's genius and foresight, Favata, the author of many texts about Colombo, recounts that during a trip to the United States with Gae Aulenti, he told her that in the future, everyone would have a telephone in their pocket, and he further added that work would also change, allowing us to work from home. Gae looked at him with a bewildered expression, but Joe continued, saying that designers wouldn't work alone with their pencils, but rather in collaboration with technicians, doctors, scientists, and professors, not to mention an electronic brain in the not-so-distant future.

When we look at Joe Colombo's objects today, we are left speechless by the visionary nature of their creator. Whether it's a chair, a lamp, or a vision, it becomes evident that he possessed the uncommon talent of giving new shape to ideas. In a way, Joe was inventing the future. He had an interest in mechanics and automobiles and nurtured a great curiosity for everything new, including materials.

The underlying idea behind Colombo's best projects was to have an environment that would adapt to people's needs rather than the other way around. Colombo has always been described as an elegant and charismatic man who managed to express his conception of Design through the use of materials accompanied by futuristic forms. He thus created adaptable, flexible objects where the shapes appeared soft, sinuous, and devoid of angles. Everything he created became somewhat iconic thanks to the new form he managed to give it. Colombo didn't stop at objects; in fact, he was able to envision and actualize an entirely new way of life.

His work on modularity should be considered revolutionary, embracing the concept of 'all-in-one.' This gave rise to televisions that emerged from ceilings, revolving walls with minibars inside, control panels to access different electronic devices and even make phone calls!

This also happened with his lamp, the KD27, a kind of tube with a luminous sphere inside, which originated from an initial 'Ready-Made' operation that the Castiglioni brothers would later utilize.

Giulio Castelli, the founder of Kartell, recounted that one day, he saw Joe Colombo carefully observing Gino Colombini's umbrella stand in Kartell's Noviglio showroom. Joe examined it from all angles, held it in his hand, and rotated it while circling around it without saying a word.

In that moment, he was envisioning something different. After some time, Colombo proposed to Castelli to produce his lamp, the KD27, which was nothing more than Colombini's umbrella stand cut in half and fitted with internal lighting. No one knows for sure, but what do you think Gino's reaction was when he saw his umbrella stand cut and put up for sale with a light bulb inside…?
Colombini never said anything about it.

Giulio Castelli

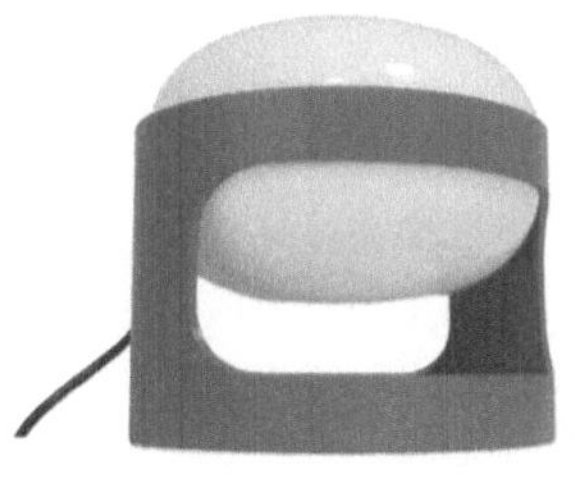

KD27 Kartell by Joe Colombo

The Kartell umbrella stand by Gino Colombini

The 1006 Navy Chair is a chair made of recycled aluminum, melted and welded into a single piece, giving it more resemblance to a sculpture than a seating. There are no screws, bolts, or joints; all the welds are seamless.

# "Joker, plop your buttocks onto that chair!!"

**Once it was said that objects lasted a lifetime, but today things are different. Often, after just two years, they start showing signs of wear. The truth is that we try to save money, which leads us to buy low-cost items that have a short lifespan. Ultimately, a quality product that withstands the test of time inevitably requires a slightly higher investment.**

During the early days of World War II, the USS Vincennes was set ablaze as soon as the bullets reached the hangar area. The damage was not considered fatal, except for the contribution of paint, objects, and life jackets, which largely fueled the fire, illuminating the sky and attracting enemy fire. At the first light of dawn on August 9, 1942, the Vincennes sank in the waters near Savo Island in the South Pacific.

There were other similar losses that prompted the U.S. Navy to launch a campaign to eliminate anything on combat ships that could catch fire. A new regulation was issued, prohibiting cork insulation, linoleum floors, carpets, and curtains. This was followed by a list of various items that sailors carried with them, essentially eliminating any excess items that could ignite. However, it was not entirely easy to remove all objects, such as wooden benches.

This provided an opportunity to issue a call for a new navy chair, which caught the attention of a young engineer from Baltimore, Wilton Dinges. The seats had to possess the following characteristics: waterproofness, strength, lightness, and corrosion resistance, without causing any magnetic interference with onboard or external systems. With the help of aluminum manufacturer Alcoa, Dinges managed to create the 1006 model weighing 7 pounds. However, due to the war and the difficulty of obtaining materials, he could only work with soft aluminum obtained from recycling scrap.

What initially seemed like a disadvantage became an advantage. By utilizing the characteristics of malleable aluminum, it became easy to create the chair's curved back, tapered legs, and distinctive molded shape. Some claim that the shape was carved based on the curves of Betty Grable's buttocks (1916-1973), a famous dancer and model of that period.

Dinges then treated the aluminum with a series of heat and acid treatments, achieving a hardness three times greater than that of steel alone. An Emeco chair certainly doesn't come cheap when considering the 77 steps required to produce it. Today, the price ranges around 800 euros for a satin chair and over 1000 euros for a polished one.

To demonstrate the strength and resilience of the 1006 chair to the Navy, Dinges performed a demonstration in a hotel room on the eighth floor in Chicago. After falling from that height, the chair landed unharmed. Thanks to this test, Dinges secured the contract and subsequently founded Emeco (Electric Machine and Equipment Company) for its production.

In 1944, the first chairs were used for equipping submarines until the end of the war. They survived kamikaze attacks and even withstood two typhoons in the Pacific. It's worth noting that when the U.S. Army tested two atomic bombs at Bikini Atoll in July 1946, the chairs inside the battleship USS Nevada were only slightly damaged by a nuclear weapon detonated at a distance of only 615 meters.

At the end of the war, Emeco built its current factory in Hanover, Pennsylvania, and continued to produce chairs for the military while expanding its business to other sectors such as restaurants, schools, and hospitals, where there was a need for furniture with clean and durable lines.

These chairs are so indestructible that they can last over 150 years. Considering what has just been said, it can be said that the 1006 chairs from World War II are reaching the midpoint of their lifespan. The popularity of this chair began to wane due to its high cost in the late 1970s when new, significantly cheaper furniture became available on the market.

Personally, I like to imagine the 1006 chair in two situations. The first relates to its intended place of use, where military personnel sit on this chair inside submarines, listening attentively as they sense magnetic mines passing by (some claim that this is one of the reasons why the chairs were made of aluminum). The second is an image that belongs to those who make the chair, so it is not difficult for me to envision old bikers with their distinctive appearance, welding all day, dirty and tough. Then in the evening, they ride home on their Harley Davidson, feeling like part of a great story.

The Navy Chair 1006 has appeared in many movies such as Matrix, Kingsman, I, Robot, and The Dark Knight. Do you remember the scene where Batman, while beating up the Joker, decides to block the exit with a 1006 chair? There is no doubt that it is a sturdy chair if even Batman used it.

From the film "The Dark Knight"
Property of Warner Bros.

# Citrus Juicer  "Spremita"
### Lino Saltini (Joseph Majewski RIVAL 1932)
### ATLANTIC 1950

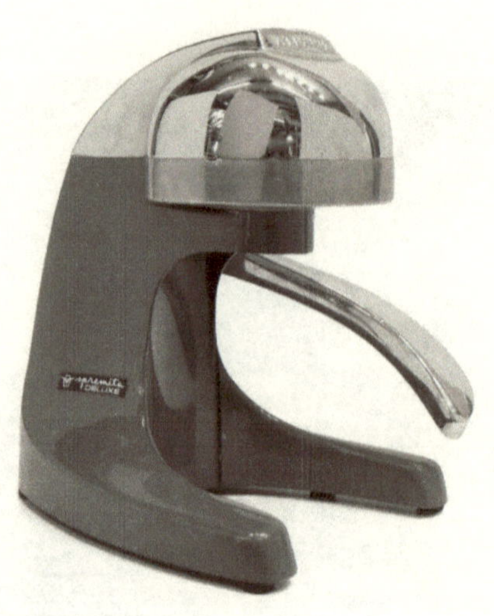

*Spremita is a heavy-duty lever citrus juicer. It consists of a crushing body made of chrome-plated iron, a cone for placing the citrus fruit, and an aluminum juice container mounted on a painted iron base. The juicer had a visually refined design, with distinct Art-Deco features initially and Streamline characteristics later on. This model is the successor to Rival's 1937 'Juice-O-Mat' (Tilt-Top model).*

# "First, have a drink, and then a quick phone call..."

**At times, the fine line between art and design becomes blurred and difficult to distinguish. Artists become designers, and designers draw inspiration from art. Creativity and functionality intertwine, blurring the boundary even further.**

A man who could be defined as an "architect-designer-artist" in every sense of the word left significant legacies in all the fields he worked in, denying or perhaps denying to be part of one or another world. This man, unknown to most, was called Lino Saltini, and he only designed two objects of which we are aware in his career as a designer: a telephone and a juicer. Saltini was a tormented artist who managed to be both an artist and a fine designer. Observing his paintings and works, one might even dare to say that they were not created by the same man, but perhaps by twin brothers who pursued completely different professions (!).

Let's go back to the late 1930s to unravel this intricate story. We are in the United States, in 1937, shortly after the discovery of vitamin C, which was being used to combat swelling, fever, anemia, gum bleeding, weight loss, muscle pains, and almost every ailment. This health craze swept across the USA with unprecedented ease, accompanied by an advertising campaign that convinced every American to drink a glass of orange juice every morning. This led to the need for assistance with juicing, something that would make the process easier. Joseph Majewski, a Polish engineer, designed a lever-operated juicer and patented it in 1939 under the name "Juice-O-Mat." He sold the patent to the Rival Manufacturing Company in Kansas City, which specialized in metal kitchenware.

The strong Art Deco lines and soft colors of the 1930s and 1940s, along with the chrome finishes on the top part of this object, reflect the era and make it easily identifiable within its time. If we move towards the 1950s, the edges and curves become softer (typically Streamline), and the colors are vibrant pink, blue, copper, and chrome. In the 1960s, the objects become more modern but still nod to the past.

Due to the fascist racial laws promulgated in Italy in 1938, an entrepreneur born in Milan emigrated to the USA in 1940 and could only return to his country after the war. We are talking about Giorgio (George) Gentilli, who came back to Italy with a commercial collaboration contract with Rival (kitchenware) and Philco (home appliances), founding Atlantic Electric in Milan. His company marketed and later produced Rival kitchen accessories, as well as refrigerators and televisions in collaboration with Philco. Gentilli's advertising campaign in magazines and on the emerging television industry helped sell thousands of juicers, renamed "Spremita," achieving incredible success in our country.

Finding it in the used market today is very easy and inexpensive due to the high number of existing pieces still available.

Towards the late 1950s, Atlantic had to suspend sales as the aluminum container would oxidize upon contact with citrus acid, and it was declared toxic. Gentilli explained the problem to Rival, who responded that they had no intention of producing a different juicer at the time. However, Gentilli didn't give up. He entrusted the restyling to the architect and painter Lino Saltini (an artist of Tuscan origin but born in Milan in 1908, with a Florentine father and Milanese mother). Saltini had already designed the famous gray S62 rotary telephone, which entered every Italian household with SIP in 1962. Instead of redesigning the juicer, Saltini maintained its design while replacing the heavy base with a thinner aluminum, eliminating the toxic metal container in favor of a glass cup, and replacing the metal juicing cone with a plastic one. Thus, the "Spremita De Luxe" was born, which became a sales success for the next 20 years.

Unfortunately, towards the late 1970s, like many other Italian companies, Atlantic was hit by the rampant economic crisis. Additionally, Gentilli's company had heavily focused on producing color models, despite something preventing the start of color broadcasting in Italy, causing a significant delay compared to other countries. While almost the entire Europe had color television by 1967, Italy was still broadcasting in black and white in the 1970s, with never-ending "color test" broadcasts. It was only in 1977 that RAI began broadcasting in color, but it was too late for Italian factories to catch up with the experience acquired by foreign competitors. Atlantic closed its doors, Gentilli retired, and Rival continued

selling kitchen products, specializing in an innovative pot: the Crock-Pot, the highlight of their catalog.
It was an innovative electric cooker with a remova-
ble glass or ceramic pot that cooked food slowly and
could be left unattended safely for hours while maintaining low temperatures. Thanks to the increasing
number of working women, this cooker quickly gained popularity in the 1970s, saving more than one
marriage. Rival continued selling this pot until 1986.
Today, Rival no longer exists, having been absorbed
by companies that produce fans and air conditioners,
perhaps unaware of the glorious past of the Kansas
City-based company. And what about Saltini? His nature was extremely rebellious and restless, much like
his adolescence. He managed to graduate from the
Brera Academy by intermittently attending day and
evening schools. He then attended the Higher School of Architecture in Valle Giulia, Rome, but swiftly
moved from one experience to another, convinced
that the practices and knowledge of minor arts are
essential for an artist: from frescoes to stained glass,
ceramics, set design, graphics, industrial design, architecture, and furniture. At the age of 23, in 1931,
he had his first press and critical success. From 1944
to 1965, he sought an aesthetic that was more in line
with the reality of his time and pursued his cultural
renewal, feeling the pressure of new trends.
The drawings, studies, travels, readings, and discussions during these twenty years, this "active intro-
spection," distanced him from art exhibitions. It was
only in 1965 that he reappeared at the Bollag Gallery
in Zurich with a collection of works, followed by a

solo exhibition at the Woodstock Gallery in London in 1966. It is worth noting that from 1944, he did not put any of his paintings or drawings up for sale. During the London exhibition, rather than selling some works requested by snobbish buyers, he decided to pay a penalty fee to the gallery instead. Saltini was also a strict destroyer of his own works. The artist intended to leave only a few works upon his death, which would summarize, through their completeness and validity, the outcome of a life dedicated to art. The most qualified art critics in history have spoken about his works, but his name will always be associated with the history of design due to the bi-gray S62 telephone from SIP and the sparkling juicer that adorned kitchens, entering the homes of millions of Italians and never leaving.

Including my own home, where it was used daily by my mother, who lovingly told me, *""My love, drink the freshly squeezed juice, it's good for you and you'll grow big." " followed by, "Are you still on the phoneeee!!!??"* out knowing it, Saltini became the joy and pain of all Italian families.

Siemens S62

**Ashtray "CUBO"**
Bruno Munari
DANESE 1957

*Cubo is an open-sided cube with a slanted metal sheet inserted to conceal its unpleasant contents. It is an extremely essential, functional, simple, and counter-trend object.*

# "Nice cube you sent me, but what is it?"

**In the creation of a new product, it is important to consider and evaluate sociological and psychological factors to ensure that it is well understood. The social context and psychological predispositions of the buyer can influence their readiness to adopt and use certain objects.**

The Cubo ashtray was created for Danese by Bruno Munari in 1957 and is currently exhibited in the permanent collections of the Museum of Modern Art in New York.
Thanks to the rational study of form, Munari designed an ashtray that is able to hide cigarette butts from sight and smell by creating a concealed container, stylistically minimal and essential.
Every small part of its shape has an explanation. The designer achieves his goal by folding a sheet of metal and inserting it inside a perfect 6x6x6 cm robust plastic cube. The space dedicated to the butts is covered by the folded parts, hiding them from view and reducing the odor.
In reality, Munari himself tells how the visually clean external shape was a psychological mistake because he did not take into account the fact that pe-

ople, not seeing the extinguished cigarettes, could not understand the function of the object, making it a mysterious object. It was for this reason that Cubo remained unsold for two or three years until Danese supported it with appropriate communication that proved effective for sales.

(Do you remember what I said earlier, that a valid object without marketing communication doesn't go anywhere? Well, this is the most striking example).

Another brilliant insight of this product is its practicality: to empty it, you just have to extract the aluminum foil and drop the contents into the trash.

After this small gesture, it can be reinserted into the cube.

In 1992, during a meeting at the University of Venice, Bruno Munari shared an anecdote about this product: a lady gifted Cubo to a friend who, by pure chance, had assembled it in reverse, making it even more cryptic than usual regarding its function. The lady then called the friend who had given it to her, saying, *"That cubic thing you sent me is beautiful, but what is it?"*.

The friend explained that it was an ashtray, and at that point, the lady asked how to use it. She received an explanation that cigarette butts could be inserted into the slit, but in her case, due to the incorrect assembly, the slit was only slightly larger than a millimeter and therefore couldn't function.

It was only after accidentally dropping the object that the lady discovered it was mounted upside down.

The design of Cubo remains relevant even today, despite dating back to 1957. The inscription "fuma dopo" (smoke later) printed by Munari on the cube adds to its contemporaneity by inviting the smoker to postpone their cigarette break without feeling restricted.

The choice to include this inscription also indicates the ironic intent of the designer, which, considering that all this was created in 1957, makes this minimal object even more unique. Throughout his career, Munari pursued the invisible essence of things, the complicated simplicity.

In this regard, he said: "*Complicating is easy, simplifying is difficult. To complicate, you just need to add anything you want: colors, shapes, actions, decorations, characters, environments filled with things. Everyone is capable of complicating. Few are capable of simplifying. To simplify, you need to remove, and to remove, you need to know what to remove, just like a sculptor who, with chisel blows, removes from the stone block all the material that is more than the sculpture he wants to create. Theoretically, every stone block can contain a beautiful sculpture inside it, so how do you know where to stop removing without ruining the sculpture? Indeed, simplification is the sign of intelligence. An ancient Chinese saying goes: 'What cannot be said in a few words cannot be said in many either'.*

# Armchair "UP5+6"
Gaetano Pesce
B&B 1969-2000

In this highly original armchair, there is an important element related to its packaging. The interior of the seat is made of expanded polyurethane, which is compressed and vacuum-sealed to reduce its volume by up to 90%. This allows the armchair to be sold in a flat form, saving on transportation and storage. Once unpacked, air enters the upholstery, causing the armchair to "inflate.

# "Just a moment... I'll flatten the chair and be right there!"

**When art and design merge, it becomes evident. Explicit forms, sometimes contorted, at times exuberant, with functionality perhaps taking a back seat. The message prevails over function. However, it is not always the case. In a functional design object, significant imaginative effort may be required to understand a particular form.**

We are talking about the 'Armchair with Ball and Chain,' which has become famous for its message of denouncing the condition of women. Only through careful observation of its form do we realize the message that designer Gaetano Pesce intended to convey with his work/chair called UP 5, an absolute masterpiece paying homage to women and part of a series of seats created from the 1960s onwards.

By closely examining the armchair, we can see the fairly explicit shape of the maternal womb. The chair is characterized by sinuous and ample forms, clear symbols of fertility: two large breasts adorn the upper part of the backrest, while the lower part resembles thighs, providing a feeling of being en-

veloped when seated, reminiscent of our childhood.
This armchair, designed in 1969 during a period of
great revolutionary fervor, continues to be produced by B&B Italia to this day.
It has been featured in many films and exhibited in
various museums, becoming one of the most well-
known icons of Italian design worldwide.
A symbol that, even after over fifty years, does not
seem to lose the power of its message.
Gaetano Pesce says: *'When I conceived the UP series, I was telling a story about my personal concept of woman: women have always been, despite
themselves, prisoners of themselves. With this in
mind, I gave this chair the shape of a woman with
a ball and chain, replacing the usual image of a
prisoner.'*
The artwork stimulates critical thinking about the
condition of women, who are still victims of preju-
dice and violence in various parts of the world, a
theme that unfortunately never goes out of fashion.
In addition to the political message, Gaetano Pesce's armchair marks a revolution in new materials
and production techniques used: without an internal structure, UP5 is made of expanded polyurethane and was vacuum-packed, reducing the space oc-
cupied during transportation and packaging.
Once unpacked, the chair would expand by absor-
bing air until it assumed its original shape.
The artist, during an interview, recounts how the
idea came to him while taking a shower: *'The idea*

for UP5 came to me while looking at a sponge in the shower. The idea was to design a chair that, like a sponge, could be compressed and become very small, only to return to its normal size.'
Speaking of art and design, British designer John Maeda said, 'Design is the solution to a problem. Art is the question underlying a problem.'"

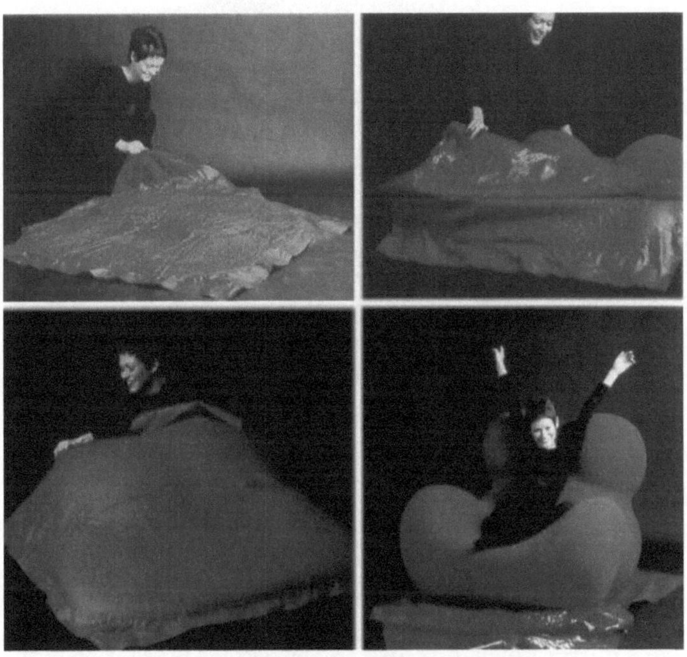

The "expansion" assembly system.
Initially, it is a flat sheet, and after opening a valve, air slowly enters, inflating the chair.

 **Wired broadcasting system "FD1102"**
Richard Sapper -Marco Zanuso
BRIONVEGA 1969

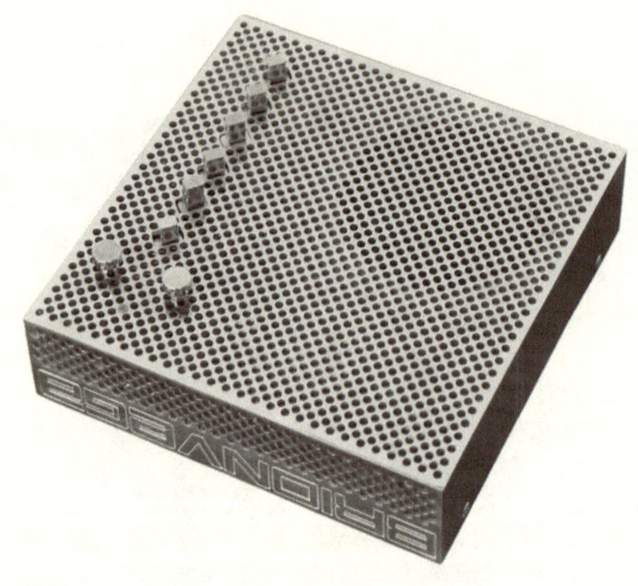

The FD 1102 model is a square-based parallelepiped made
of sheet metal, which is cut, bent, and then chrome-plated
to a mirror finish. The logo "Brionvega" is present on both
sides. It features six rectangular colored buttons for the six
channels of the wired radio transmission system, as well
as two round knobs for volume control and power. It is a
marvelous piece with an apparent simplicity.

# "Did you print the logo upside down by any chance...?"

**Often, it is difficult to explain in detail the design choices, considering that a designer carefully crafts every millimeter of the object, and sometimes even they themselves do not know why they have adopted a specific form. One wonders if there is a "right" form for an object. Should it be long or perhaps short? Should the angles be more or less curved? Every creative act generates countless questions.**

The questions for a designer are an integral part of their sleepless nights, spent chasing one question after another, when suddenly a little voice, somewhat similar to that of the Jedi Master Yoda from Star Wars, comes out of nowhere, repeating, *"Form Follows Function... Form Follows Function... Follow the force, or rather, follow the form..."*

*"Form follows function"* is the clear answer to the question of the shape that the object we are designing should have.

This phrase was not uttered by Master Yoda, but is a principle coined by architect Louis Sullivan in 1896. Initially applied to modern architecture of the 20th century, it later extended to industrial design.

The principle asserts that the form of an object should follow the purpose or function for which it is created, rather than merely covering a structure.

Designers Marco Zanuso and Richard Sapper, the

former Italian and the latter German, managed to create a design partnership that lasted for thirty years. Thanks to this collaboration, they gifted us with unforgettable objects that have won numerous awards even to this day.

The famous Ts 502 Cube Radio and the Doney and Algol televisions by Brionvega, and the Grillo telephone, are all well remembered by everyone.

Less known to most is undoubtedly the FD1102 wired radio by Brionvega, a chrome-plated metal parallelepiped with a mirrored surface.

Wired radio broadcasting is practically non-existent today, but forty years ago, radio was distributed through a telecommunications network that directly reached users' homes using the telephone wires that connected buildings with fixed telephony.

The FD1102 wired radio they created was without too many compromises, thanks to its primitive and essential form, where the only element of movement was provided by the contrast of the metal, the austere-shaped buttons, and the remarkable Brionvega logo, considering its dimensions.

There is a particular detail related to the logo that not everyone notices: the Brionvega logo is straight on one side and rotated 180° upside down on the other side.

At first glance, it may seem like a production mistake, but in reality, it reveals the functionalist and pragmatic thinking of its creators, where form follows function and not the other way around.

The reason is quite simple: if you place the radio on its side or attach it to a wall, the logo becomes readable from bottom to top. It's a simple yet brilliant insight.

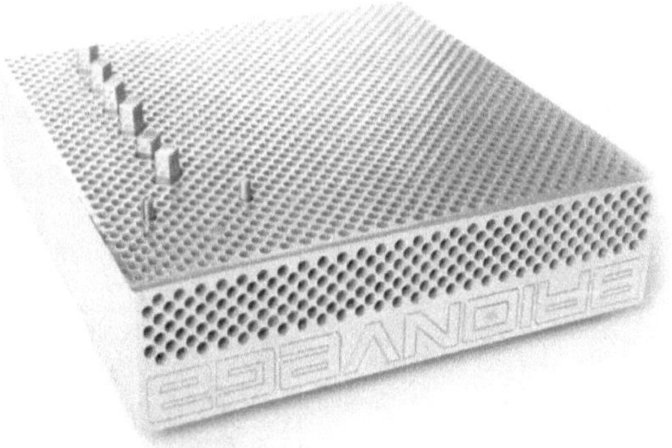

The wired broadcasting system where the "BRIONVEGA" logo is seen reversed.

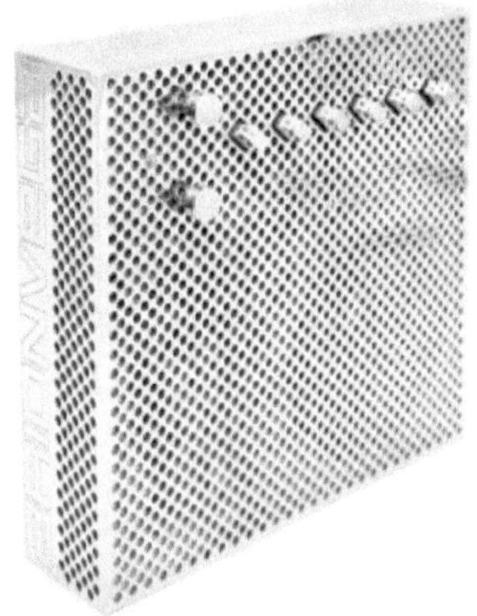

Once placed upright, the logo becomes "correct" and readable from bottom to top.

# Bookcase "Carlton"
Ettore Sottsass
MEMPHIS 1981

Upon closer inspection, this bookcase indeed has a distinctly anthropomorphic shape, resembling a person with raised arms and spread legs. Carlton is a composition of primitive geometric shapes, colored and stacked on top of each other, resembling large pixels in a video game.

# "If you have a living room that is 500 square meters, it's perfect."

**Creating a new style involves surpassing the creative limits imposed by the industry, introducing innovative forms, materials, and stimuli in design. This concept must be deeply ingrained in the mind of every designer.**

How else could we define the architect and designer Ettore Sottsass, if not as a poet, a rebel, a versatile artist, cool, a lover of travel, and a friend to personalities like Hemingway, Picasso, and Allen Ginsberg? His creations have encompassed the first computers, from Olivetti to reaching the Silicon Valley in the USA. He didn't stop at technology but also dedicated himself to fashion with Fiorucci and to objects with Alessi.

Ettore Sottsass and Barbara Radice arrive in a taxi at the Arc '74 gallery in Milan on September 18, 1981. They are both excited and somewhat anxious for the opening of the exhibition of domestic furnishing objects by Memphis, the group created by Ettore just a year before, which would revolutionize the future of design in just a few years.

The goal was to break free from the cold colors combined with the monochrome of the 1970s in terms of design, thanks to new concepts drawn from the past.

When Ettore and Barbara arrived at the exhibition, they were amazed by the number of people waiting outside the showroom. At first, they thought someone had fallen ill and that most of the crowd had gathered to see what was happening. In truth, all those people were there to see the furniture, lamps, ceramics, and whatever else they had created.

Until then, no design event had managed to bring together so many people. The invitation card for the exhibition featured a Tyrannosaurus Rex with its mouth wide open, white teeth, and a vivid eye, so realistic.

An invitation that became a suggestive communication vehicle, to the point of wondering: *will Memphis, like a dinosaur, devour modern design?* Well, yes, the group led by Sottsass, composed among others of Alessandro Mendini, Michele De Lucchi, Aldo Cibic, Matteo Thun, Marco Zanini, Martine Bedin, and Andrea Branzi, did exactly that.

Memphis represented the forge of desires, where previously unknown emotions were born.

One element of that exhibition, to the point of becoming a symbol, was the Carlton bookcase (all the products from the first collection of 1981 were named after important hotels: Plaza, Casablanca, D'Antibea, Pierre, and Carlton), designed and created by Ettore Sottsass in 1981 for Memphis.

Upon careful observation, one notices the unique shelving that can also serve as a room divider. It certainly adds value beyond the classical concept of a bookcase against a wall.

Its functionality appears reduced when considering the inclined shelves. The design intention was not merely to create a bookcase but rather to combine it with a work of art.

Colors dance in a kitsch and grotesque play, accompanied by the choice to employ poor materials such as colored laminate, as a protest against rampant consumerism. In the early 1960s, Sottsass traveled to India and was fascinated by the clothing and houses with their vibrant colors. This was the starting point where he understood the importance of color.

Many refer to it as the "Totem" bookcase due to its shape, which resembles a person with raised arms and spread legs.

It consists of inclined planes on both the right and left sides, with a chest of drawers placed at the bottom resting on a black and white parallelepiped. It is certainly not small, considering its four-meter size and significant weight exceeding a quintal.

Carlton became the iconic piece of the entire movement, to the extent that Sottsass himself declared that he created these furniture pieces as a form of protest against bourgeois furnishings.

Carlton is unique to the point where it can stand alone like a monument in a large square. The only caution is to have a living room as spacious as a parade ground...

# Piano "Pegasus"
Lutz Colani
SCHIMMEL 1997

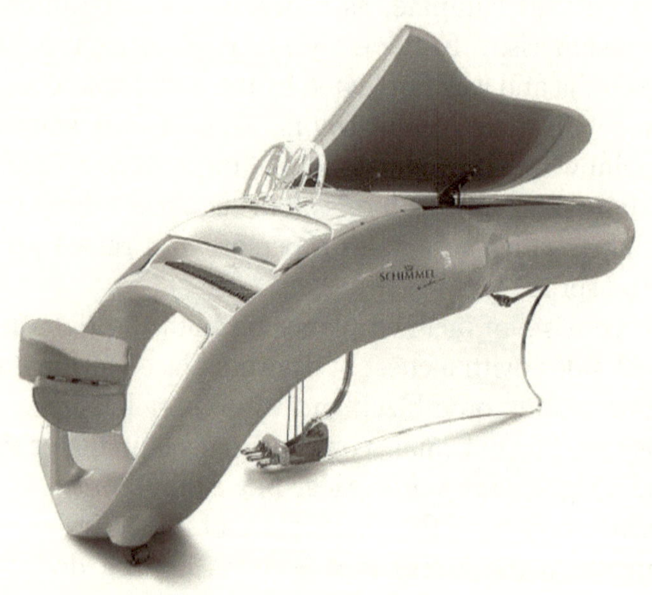

*Pegasus is a futuristic and highly elegant piano designed by Lutz Colani. Curvaceous like an organic form, it is made from a single piece of fiberglass without any joints. Even the keyboard is unique, as it is not straight but slightly curved. Pegasus is exhibited at the Museum of Modern Art in New York.*

# "But it's all a curve... There isn't a straight line?"

**Nature, with its sinuous and complex forms, often inspires designers. Whether it's a piano, a car, or a water bottle, the beauty of nature always offers new forms that evoke wonder.**

Luigi (Lutz) Colani was indeed a highly unconventional and visionary designer. Known for his unique and organic design approach, he pushed the boundaries of traditional forms and embraced curved lines and aerodynamics in his creations. Some even likened him to an alien, as his designs deviated from the ordinary and drew inspiration from organic curves and biodynamics.

Colani was versatile in his design pursuits, ranging from cars with long and streamlined bodies to televisions, clothing, cameras, eyewear, and furniture, all characterized by their rounded shapes.

He believed in a supernatural world where forms could capture both violence and sensuality.

Throughout his career, he remained true to his design sensibility, leveraging principles of physics and observing nature to inform his designs.

One of Colani's most notable works is the Canon T90 camera, as well as the chaise longue designed for Kusch. However, it's important to note that mentioning just a couple of his works is limiting, considering he created over 4,000 products throughout his career.

In 1997, Colani collaborated with German piano manufacturer Schimmel Pianos to design the Pegasus grand piano, a project that revolutionized the very form of pianos.

The Pegasus, a limited edition grand piano measuring approximately 6 feet 10 inches (208 cm), features a distinctly organic shape, with even the keyboard following the same logic.

When the first Pegasus was unveiled in 1997, it initially received mixed reactions, with some considering it frivolous.

However, over time, the design of the Pegasus gained appreciation and recognition as a design classic. The Pegasus is a monolithic instrument that includes an extendable and adjustable stool, addressing the diverse needs of pianists in terms of height, position, and distance from the keyboard. It eschews traditional legs, giving it a suspended appearance.

The body is made of fiberglass, with continuous wave-like lines creating a sense of fluidity. The hydraulic lid with electric control adds to its adjustability. And of course, the iconic Pegasus winged horse statuette is a delightful touch.

Schimmel continues to produce no more than two Pegasus pianos each year, exclusively by order. Only a select few celebrities own this grand piano, including Prince, Lenny Kravitz, and Eddy Murphy, to name a few.

It's hard to definitively categorize Colani as either a lucid genius or a visionary madman. He was undoubtedly a unique individual, and his creations displayed a touch of otherworldliness.

To truly appreciate the breadth and impact of his work, it's recommended to explore his designs online and witness his extraordinary creations firsthand.

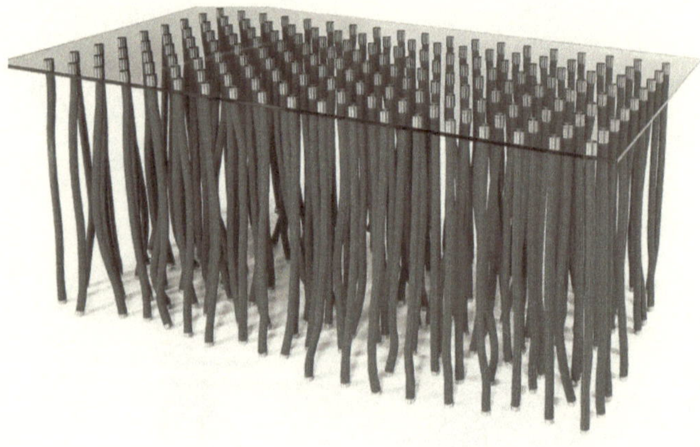

The Org table, composed of a glass top and 171 red rope legs, represents a clear provocation as the table appears to float in the air. In reality, among the rope legs, there are 4 steel legs covered in red rope that conceal a magical effect.

# "Hide yourself there underneath, quickly, I designed it on purpose."

**As stated by the famous American graphic designer Milton Glaser, when faced with an object of design, we can react with three possible responses: "yes," "no," and "wow!". However, to achieve success, it is essential that the object elicits an exciting reaction from the very first encounter, an authentic "wow."**

Every time we come across a strange object, it is legitimate to wonder whether it is art or design. Regarding this magical table, I would say that its strangeness lies in the number of its legs, one hundred and seventy-one. However, in an industrial product, it must be said that no matter how strange it is, it should provide a coherent answer in terms of form and function.

*"In spite of all efforts, the kind smile that appears on a mother's face when conversations become more complex always has the same meaning it had since childhood: 'Are you hungry, Fabio? Have you eaten? Shall I prepare something for you?'".*

Fabio Novembre, in his book *"Il Design spiegato a mia madre"* ("Design Explained to My Mother"), quotes this sentence while writing that it is difficult to explain to his own mother (and I believe to any mother of a creative person) why he designed a table with all those legs.

It must be said that there is an explanation, even though at first glance, Fabio's Org table approaches an almost magical paradox. The upper part of the table seems to rest on elements that rain down from above, resembling tendrils thanks to their flexibility and the fact that they are made of red polypropylene rope, among four rigid legs with a steel core and an outer rope to hide the trick.

Fabio Novembre, a Lecce-born artist born in 1966, was a student of the highly visionary designer Ettore Sottsass, to the extent that he has been defined as a Pop artist.

If you notice, the term "artist" was used instead of "designer." This definition was well received because, for him, his work also meant staying close to people's dreams.

How could we define a designer capable of interpreting dreams, thus bringing people's tastes closer to pleasant creations that also contain a deeper message?

A pure creative like Fabio has stated that, for him, the act of designing objects is a way to avoid falling into the unknown and to overcome his fears.

This table evokes the idea of a hiding place; it is said that this intuition came to him when he hid under the table at his girlfriend's house after an unexpected return of her parents. (...)

The Org table, with its numerous legs, demonstrates

that the designer was more interested in what happened under the table than above it. I believe that this object belongs to a more "artistic" fringe than to design because it lacks a strong utilitarian motivation. We have seen many objects that provoke "wow" effects in the last 60 years; today, they can still elicit this sensation, but it is precisely old stuff. This object lacks one of the central pillars of design, which is functionality. Try cleaning all the legs of the table, and you will discover that it will neither be comfortable nor easy.

However, as in the case of Starck's juicer, where the object acquires an industrial value only when its intended use is changed (from a juicer to a "conversation piece"), the discourse magically shifts.

If Fabio claimed that he designed the intricate shadowy legs precisely to hide and that his mysterious legs are perfect for hiding without the fear of being discovered, then it would be worth some sacrifice, and it would rightfully return to being a "design" object by solving the problem of where to hide the lover in case the partner unexpectedly returns home.

**Lamp "Gun"**
Philippe Starck
FLOS 2005

A classic lampshade with an AK-47 assault rifle as its stem.
Gold-plated. In the same series, there is also a pistol.

# "Our life is worth nothing but a bullet..."

**The design object can be used as a vehicle to convey a political concept or to express a message of denunciation.**

Philippe Starck's journey in the world of design began with his attendance at the prestigious private institute for interior and product design, École Nissim de Camondo. However, he was not particularly exceptional in school and often tried to avoid attending. His genius, characterized by ironic and sumptuous details, good taste, and madness, started to emerge during his time at the institute. His early works focused on interior design for homes, establishments, hotels, and even a spaceship, all reflecting his unique style.

In 1986, Philippe Starck embarked on an unstoppable sequence of design pieces for the home, with his studio providing an official list that spans an impressive 13 pages. Beyond household objects, he has designed various types of products, ranging from boats to televisions, and he has even personally curated a blend for a champagne. Love and desire are foundational concepts in Philippe Starck's approach to design, as he recognizes the ambitious task of *"improving the lives of as many people as possible."*

His vision is inclusive and optimistic, aiming to align with the ideals of recognized Italian masters such as Achille Castiglioni, to whom he explicitly acknowledges his debt.

Regarding the relationship between form and function (understood as a role in a broader sense) in the designed object, Starck reflected on the need to replace beauty, which he considers a cultural concept, with goodness—a humanistic concept—in a conversation with Elizabeth Laville in 1998.

In an interview with Corriere della Sera, his vibrant personality shines through. He owns eighteen properties scattered across the globe, from Ibiza to New York, the Atlantic, and the island of Burano, all furnished identically, even down to the books, creating a consistently comforting environment every time he crosses the threshold. He adheres to a strict personal discipline, not only in terms of diet (black bread, honey, dried fruit, and herbal tea for breakfast) but also in the scheduling of his days, meticulously planned down to the minute with back-to-back meetings and visits to clients, sometimes up to three in different countries, all made possible by his private jet. He approaches his projects with methodical precision, drawing each one in meticulous detail on tracing paper, which he guards jealously.

As we have always stated, one of the essential characteristics of design is that an object carries functionality, as well as innovation, utility, and beauty—it should meet specific criteria for which it has been designed. In the case of the "Gun" lamp, the initial impression may suggest a somewhat kitschy object—a style associated with presumed artistic objects of poor taste. However, Philippe Starck's primary intention is not to create a common and tasteless lighting object. Instead, he aims to denounce the arms trade and the warmongering greed of the modern world. The provocative, symbolic, polemic, and subversive nature of the "Gun" lamp serves as a statement against the arms trade. Its precious chrome or 18-carat gold finish reveals the collusion between money and war, all while fulfilling its function with minimal effort. A portion of the proceeds from the Guns collection goes to the Frère des Hommes Europe association, which fights against poverty worldwide.

Although I generally do not favor politicized design, I admit to being captivated by Philippe Starck's all-encompassing creative and exuberant charm, so I turn a blind eye.

## Cahir "Cantilever"

Mart Stam, Ludwig Mies Van Der Rohe, Marcel Breuer.
Thonet-Standard Mobel- Desda
1926-1927

Stam

Mies

Breuer

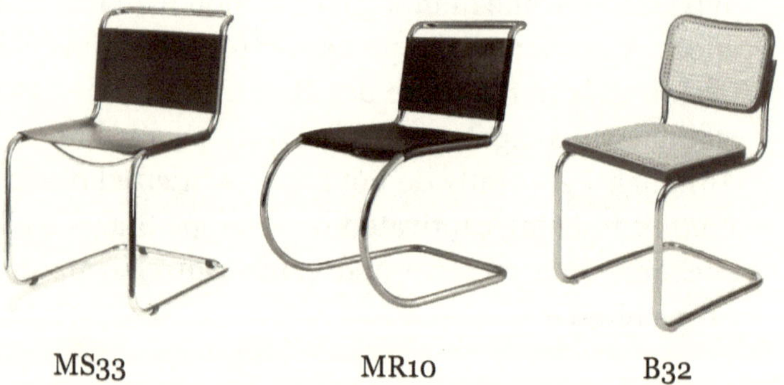

MS33

MR10

B32

This extraordinary chair, called the "cantilever" chair, is a
true masterpiece of engineering. It is a chair without rear
legs, an extraordinary object that offers effective comfort,
making anyone who sits in it feel as if they are suspended in
mid-air.

# "So who invented it in the end?..."

**Often, even in the projects of the most famous design objects, it is difficult to establish a clear boundary between the origin of the idea and its realization, especially when several people are closely involved.**

This is a very intricate and captivating story shrouded in mystery, beginning without a clearly defined starting point, with the initial protagonists sometimes wrapped in anonymity.

The facts: in 1926, Mart Stam presented his pioneering "Cantilever" or "floating" chair without rear legs, named MS 33, characterized by a rigid metal tubular structure.

The following year (1927), Ludwig Mies Van der Rohe introduced a more flexible seat with his elegant MR 10. In 1928, Marcel Breuer made further improvements with his B32, based on the successes of his famous "B3" chair with chromed tubes, known as the "Wassily" chair.

The mystery of who had the original idea for this famous chair remains unsolved.

Four central figures clearly emerge: the aforementioned architects Mart Stam, Marcel Breuer, and Ludwig Mies van der Rohe. All three knew each other as they had collaborated with the famous Bauhaus school, along with the fourth protagonist of this story, Professor Gerhard Stüttgen of the Cologne Art School. This quartet of visionaries uniquely contributed to shaping this extraordinary project.

The use of steel tubing represented a revolution in furniture development, bringing an aesthetic approach never before seen. Before the introduction of steel tubes, metal structures were primarily welded, resulting in fragile and heavy pieces that easily broke when bent. In 1895, the Mannesmann brothers developed the cold drawing process, revolutionizing the production of tubes, making them strong, lightweight, and economical, suitable for various industrial applications. These tubes found success in several sectors, including engineering and automotive, and were initially used in hospitals due to their ease of cleaning.

Let's delve into the heart of the story. In 1923, Gerhard Stüttgen presented a bold cantilever chair made with Mannesmann tubes. The idea of creating a chair with a frame without rear legs emerged during a lesson on curved tube processing. Using a simple wooden shelf, Stüttgen created a more or less "S" shape, eliminating the need for traditional rear legs. However, despite the ingenuity of this concept, its innovative nature failed to capture the desired attention. The prototype, although brilliant, was dismantled in 1926, lacking any written or illustrated documentation to confirm its existence.

What we can deduce about Stüttgen's idea is that it

bore significant similarities to the "B9" stool designed by Breuer for the Bauhaus canteen in 1925. Although it was a stool and not a cantilever chair, the
curves of the tubes were strikingly similar to those
used by Stüttgen. It is perhaps reasonable to suppose
that someone, or even Stüttgen himself, might have
known or heard about this stool made with metal tubes. This remains purely a hypothesis, a speculation
that attempts to bring some rational coherence to
the intertwining of the whole story.
In 1926, Stam undertook further development of the
cantilever chair concept. His goal was ambitious: to
create a chair with an essential and efficient design,
a sort of metal tube response to the famous Thonet
No. 14 chair, known for its bent wood structure. Contrary to the idea of flexible or oscillating seats, Stam
focused on seeking a formal harmony between the
chair and its distinctive architectural style. In this
context, since the project's design shared significant
similarities with Breuer's stool and Stüttgen's chair,
the hypothesis arises that Stam might have drawn
inspiration from these sources.
To achieve the desired aesthetics, Stam made a prototype with eight gas pipes and eight elbow joints.
Today, we can see this prototype thanks to a reconstruction from 1985 (the original was dismantled
by Stam himself in the 1920s). In this increasingly complex plot, a turning point based on objective facts emerges: November 22, 1926, at the Hotel
Marquardt in Stuttgart. Sixteen architects gathered
to outline the foundations of a bold project: the cre-

ation of an avant-garde residential neighborhood in Stuttgart by 1927. In this significant context, prominent figures such as Stam and the already famous German architect Mies van Der Rohe emerged.

According to the account of architect Heinz Rasch, who was present at the table, he said that at one point, Stam, with a quick sketch on the back of a wedding invitation, presented to Mies his bold vision: a suspended chair intended to furnish the entire series of residences he had been entrusted with. It is presumed that Stam drew the prototype made with gas pipes, as Mies noted its rigid structure.

The brilliance of Stam's project enlightened Mies, who embraced its enormous potential, perfecting it by adding that element of elasticity and elegance (curved legs) that would bring fame to this creation. It is important to emphasize that Mies did not merely emulate Stam but further refined the concept, focusing on the comfort component.

After the meeting with Stam, Mies was deeply impressed by the sketch, confirmed by Sergius Ruegenberg, Mies's assistant, who stated in 1985: "Mies returned from Stuttgart in November 1926 and told us about Stam's idea for an innovative chair without rear legs. We had a drafting table hanging on the wall, and Mies drew Stam's chair on it. He even added the fittings and then said, 'These fittings are really ugly. If only they were rounded - here, that looks better,' and he drew a curve. A simple curve made by his hand over Stam's sketch transformed the chair into a new creation!" It should be noted that Stam had a genuine aversion to curved forms, which limited his development of the tubular steel chair design, precluding him from accessing greater elasticity suitable for the tubular material.

Marcel Breuer, the last protagonist of this intricate story, had the opportunity to personally admire both Stam's and Mies's creations during the Stuttgart exhibition in 1927. However, two years earlier in 1925, as previously mentioned, Breuer had already created the "B9" stool for the Bauhaus canteen and in 1925 the "Wassily" chair, the famous "Club" chair made entirely of steel tubes and black leather with a vaguely cubic shape. Finally, Breuer developed another model, initially called "B32" and later renamed "Cesca," in honor of his adopted daughter Francesca, equipping the seat and backrest with Vienna straw.

Due to the similarity between the chair's design and those previously designed by Van der Rohe and Stam, Breuer's B32 faced several legal issues. This tortuous legal path is documented in an in-depth analysis published on the Victoria and Albert Museum website in London: "As a result of a complex series of legal cases, Breuer was denied the right to claim the B32 as his own design. Discouraged by the legal actions and the idea of ending up in court, Breuer abandoned the idea of designing with tubular steel. When the court finally issued its ruling in 1932, Stam obtained the exclusive right to produce all straight-legged chairs with only two legs, including the B32. Stam's name thus replaced Breuer's in Thonet's catalogs, the company that had acquired the production rights."

We can certainly affirm that the entire journey originated from the innovation of Mannesmann tubes in 1895; the rest is conjecture. Initially, Gerhard Stüttgen, perhaps inspired by Breuer's stool, envisioned a cantilevered seat based on the concept of the springloaded seats of the 1920s cars in 1924.

In 1925, Stam, possibly having heard of or more likely having become aware of Stüttgen's seat, conceived a first prototype of a cantilever chair in a still-primitive form, making a prototype with gas pipes. In 1926, during a conversation with Ludwig Mies van der Rohe, Stam presented his project, which Mies masterfully reworked, giving the idea the refined elegance we recognize today. Finally, in 1928, Breuer developed his own model of a cantilever chair but went further by proudly claiming the basic idea of using tubes for furniture. It should be emphasized that this reconstruction remains purely hypothetical, awaiting further discoveries that may shed light on one of the most intricate cases in design history. Today, nearly a century after its inception, the chair remains shrouded in an enigmatic allure regarding who the true pioneer of the innovative cantilever chair idea was.

This work has become an icon of the modern movement and its ideals, solidifying over time as one of the most beloved and sought-after design objects worldwide.

"Stool 'B9' 1927 made by Breuer for the Bauhaus canteen."

Chair "B3" (Wassily) by Breuer

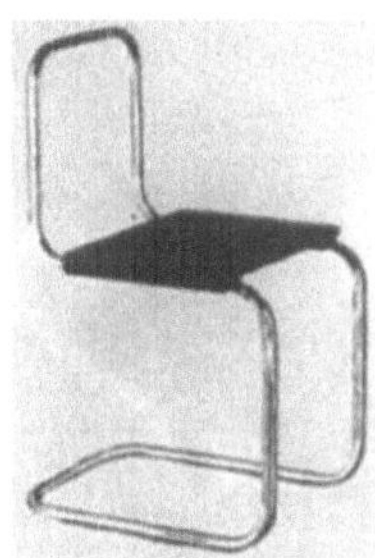

Reconstruction of Gerhard Stüttgen's chair in 1951

# Fragments of Design History

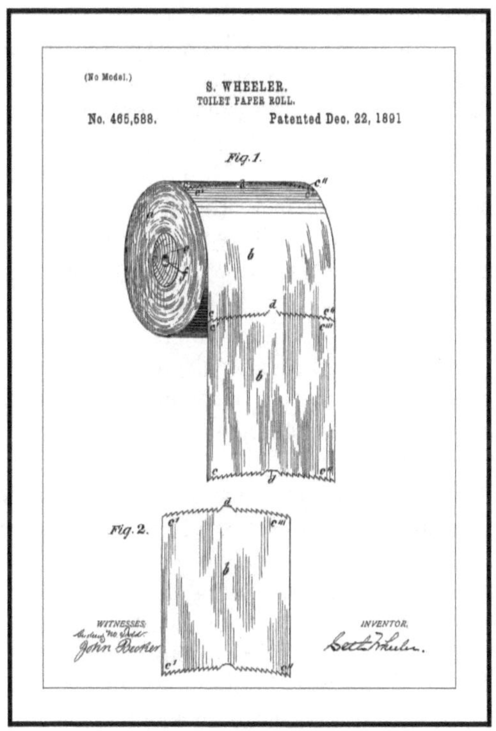



*"Recognizing the need is
the primary condition of Design."
(Charles Eames)"*

**The dawn of Design**

**-3.000.000** Paleontologists claim that for over 3 million years, humans have been inventing artifacts. In 2010, fossils of animals, along with the remains of a child, were discovered in Turkan, Kenya. These fossils appeared to have been worked with stone tools.

Today, we can affirm that those who worked those rocks were similar to Lucy or a Kenyanthropus, an early human species that lived in those regions and is considered by paleontologists as a variety of Australopithecus afarensis.

Even before the appearance of Homo sapiens, there were already hominids capable of working with stone to create objects for specific purposes. If we want to find a correlation between this history and Design, we can say that Design was born before humans.

Explaining the birth of this discipline is not entirely simple, especially because it requires analyzing various elements corresponding to the evolution of society and the individual. Human desires and needs change based on everything that surrounds their existence.

Objects speak of us and represent us. Upon careful observation, we can read not only the story of the individual but also that of the society in which they live.

While Design involves the designing of objects on one hand, on the other hand, its history allows us to journey through the history of humanity through various facets.

From prehistory onwards, humans construct objects for specific purposes. Initially, these objects have a rudimentary appearance, but over time, they undergo more and more modifications.

These same objects become increasingly functional. It can be said that through experience and transmitted knowledge, humans refine their techniques, leading to craftsmanship and the use of various materials.

Over the centuries, the craft of artisans sees the emergence of guilds, where different artisans come together to work collaboratively.

## Handicrafts

**1750** The concept of paid labor began with the first Industrial Revolution, which took place approximately between 1750 and 1830. Prior to this significant development, work was primarily a group or individual artisanal activity carried out within the home, where knowledge was passed down from father to son through simple and ancient tools.

The Industrial Revolution introduced mechanized industry with diverse production aimed at different markets. During this transition, work became collective rather than individual, controlled and organized. People operated through machines, which incorporated skills that were once reserved for artisans alone. Machines didn't need to rest, so work became continuous and organized on grueling shifts.

The factory, in a way, also transformed society, the way of life, and consumption. These changes marked the birth of the modern age. There was a rapid shift to a different lifestyle, where previously owned items were repaired or exchanged, but now the focus shifted towards consumption, and things that were no longer functional were discarded. Even today, everything we use has a short lifespan.

We barely get accustomed to one cellphone before desiring a new one.

This "modernity" entices us with its trends and fashions, and following this path leads to compulsive buying, filling our attics or landfills with things we no longer need.

The factory also changed the conception of production, labor, and, importantly, the relationship between work and the individual.

These transformations did not happen overnight but over the years. Initially, factories and craftsmanship coexisted, at least until artisans realized that it was no longer profitable to work for the masses.

Many artisans went to work in factories, while others maintained their workshops but aimed for a high standard reserved for those who had money to spend.

With the advent of machines, everything changed. A production cycle was established where each worker focused on a small part of the process, streamlining it, making it faster and less costly, resulting in lower prices.
This made it possible for even less affluent people to afford what was previously considered a luxury.
The entrepreneur emerged as a new social figure. In their pursuit of profit, they invested their capital to transform it into goods.
They monitored, organized, and directed the production process through their collaborators. Being an entrepreneur requires a mindset that promotes innovation. Sometimes, calculations and rationality are necessary, but over time, they have been associated with exploitative practices.

**Entering a factory**
**1850** Industrialization brings about another social change, as the increasing demand for work from cities leads rural populations to migrate, attracted by the greater job opportunities available. Most of these early consumers of industrial products were mostly peasants or people with little sense of aesthetics, more oriented towards the functionality and simplicity of an object. The industry aligns with this sentiment by producing simple objects, similar to those used in the past but with less aesthetic sense. Although the object was the same, there were differences between those produced by the artisan in the workshop and the factory. In the workshop, non-standardized objects with possible imperfections were created. In the factory, starting from a model, all the produced objects were identical and had no differences among them. To optimize production, more people were employed on a production line, specializing and making the entire process more efficient. Initially, mass production was not very precise, but the industrialists did not care much about it. The final product had to be simple and useful, with a lower market price to be attractive and desirable to customers.
At the beginning of the century, Giuseppe Gaetano Descal-

zi from Chiavari produced a lightweight and durable chair, albeit somewhat expensive, known as the Chiavarina. A few years later, Michael Thonet's chair, the "Number 14," entered the market and changed everything. It had the same characteristics as the Chiavarina, with the difference of being produced entirely industrially, which was crucial for cost reduction, so much so that it managed to supplant Descalzi's chair, which went out of production a few years later.

The factory's work system also led to the first agitations due to harsh working conditions and the resulting social transformations. The protests that arose were violent, despite the repressive policies adopted in some states like England.

The workers never stopped protesting to obtain their demands; they sought, then as now, to assert their point of view and not just that of profit-oriented industrialists.

## Arts and crafts

**1850** In this early period of the emerging industrial production characterized by a lack of aesthetic care, we witness the development of the Art & Craft movement by William Morris, in which he seeks to promote a return to craftsmanship, synonymous with higher quality compared to the factory production logic.

Those who worked in factories were subjected to exhausting rhythms, where any form of protection did not exist, not to mention the unhealthy environment inside and outside those walls, which promoted a precarious existence. Serial production saw the birth of various stylistic movements throughout Europe, and it was impossible to stop it.

The possibility of travel and the circulation of new ideas allowed an unprecedented cultural exchange, even with distant countries like Japan.

The new trade routes with Japan allowed the introduction of previously unknown Oriental models.

Morris' thinking regarding the aesthetically curated and high-quality object served as a pioneer in the field of Design. This conception could be defined as a bridge between craftsmanship and modern movements.

Morris' armchairs were sought after for their fabrics and patterns, and while they were industrial products, their production remained limited to a few specimens.
Morris himself once said in an interview that soon we would all become slaves to industrial production:
*"I do not say that we must strive to abolish all machines; I would like to have some things now made by hand be made by machines, and some things now made by machines be made by hand; in short, we should be masters of our machines, not slaves, as we are now."*


## Ornamentation
**1900** Towards the end of the 19th century, a new artistic style inspired by nature emerged in both architecture and decorative arts, known as Art Nouveau. This style could assume different names depending on the country.
In England, it was called Liberty; in Italy, Stile Floreale; Sapin in Switzerland; Jugendstil in Germany; Arte Jóven in Spain; and Sezessionstil in Austria.
France was the only country to resist this style to some extent, as it was mainly expressed in architecture and urban design. In France, it was referred to as Modern Style or Style Metrò, the latter term referring to the entrances of the Paris metro, which were adorned with abundant vegetal-inspired decorations and were designed by architect Hector Guimard between 1889 and 1904.
The balance between form and functionality was the primary objective of architects and designers during this period.
Art Nouveau emphasized the dominance of natural forms as sources of inspiration.
It was not only an artistic movement but also a philosophical one, where society not only embraced new forms but also accepted the increasing mass production.
Through Art Nouveau, it became possible to experiment with new materials while maintaining a craft-based production approach and an openness towards new technologies and experimentation.

In general, this movement is considered "ornamentation" that emerges from the body of the structure rather than being applied as a decorative element afterward.
Therefore, it was not negatively perceived as mere ornamentation but rather integrated from the beginning.
The movements of the post-war period managed to resist, but it was in Germany that the real turning point occurred.
Towards the end of the 19th century, Art Nouveau gained popularity throughout Europe.
Different countries embraced their own variations of the style due to their diverse cultures.
However, there were common elements such as curved lines, the presence of flowers, natural motifs, and depictions of women with long hair flowing in the wind.
The arrival of historical avant-gardes and later the modernist movement in architecture led to a negative judgment of Art Nouveau, although it was reevaluated starting in the 1950s, emphasizing its most original aspects related to design and architecture.
Nevertheless, the true groundbreaking innovation of the early 20th century undoubtedly came with the advent of electric power.


**The art of symmetry**

**1910** La simmetry with its simple and linear style stands in stark contrast to the Liberty style. The elegant and timeless taste belongs to decorative art and can be found in the furniture that characterized our childhood, also known as Art Deco.
Contrary to popular belief, this style did not originate after the war. Its conception began in 1910 thanks to the Parisian designer Paul Poiret, who aimed for an aesthetic reform of the fashion of that time.
Although it was born in those years, it became more well-known after the end of World War I, thanks to the bourgeoisie's desire to quickly forget the horrors of war.

It remained popular until the 1930s in Europe and the 1940s in America.

The Art Deco style drew inspiration from Egyptian, Chinese, and pre-Columbian civilizations, without forgetting influences from Cubism and Futurism.

It was a change that involved not only furniture but also decorative arts, architecture, and fashion.

However, it was only in 1925 that it was officially named Art Deco, thanks to the Exposition Internationale des Arts Décoratifs et Industriels Modernes held in Paris.

For this reason, many refer to it as the "Style 1925". It was during this time that the style started to decline as furniture production became more industrialized for mass consumption, diminishing its initial sense of exclusivity.

In other countries, the decline was somewhat slower, and Art Deco became the starting point for modernism.

In the 1980s, there was a revival of this style, driven by cinema, graphic design, and the fashion of the 1930s.

The main characteristic of Art Deco was given by its symmetric and geometric forms.

Although its duration did not exceed ten years, it is important to emphasize that it left a significant mark in the search for different aesthetics.

In fact, it has never gone out of fashion, as it can still be found in modern environments today.


**The Arts Campus**

**1920** The stated objective of the Bauhaus was to promote community through art, and one of its dreams was to serve the "new man" through applied art.

Walter Gropius, the founder and director of the Bauhaus, aimed to interweave different arts in order to adapt objects to various production processes, with the goal of making good design available to people in Germany after the destruction of World War I.

In our imagination, we might envision this artistic reality as a peaceful community, but in truth, the reality in Weimar was anything but peaceful. In a statement, painter Josef Albers emphasized that there was nothing on which everyone completely agreed.

If Vasily Kandinsky said yes, Josef Albers said no, and so on. Gropius desired this artistic confusion because the true objective of the Bauhaus was not to have a common dogma, but rather to rediscover fluidity in the concept of life itself. The Bauhaus was not a refuge where artists only had geometric forms in mind; the movement served as an inspiration not only for design but also for costume parties, dance evenings, and theater.

Chairs had always been made of wood, dusty, with heavy fabrics and horsehair upholstery on the inside, difficult to clean and expensive.

During that period, futuristic tubular steel chairs were designed, the same ones we still see in many offices or homes today. They were lightweight, inexpensive, and easy to clean. It was modernity in the 1920s and still is today—an iconic "long-seller" that is timeless.

The Bauhaus was a school that later became a global reference for design, not only in the development of products but also in organizing exhibitions and more. They designed over 1,000 products, including chairs, armchairs, lamps, teapots, toys, and carpets. It was probably the first (and largest) design school in the world.

In 1933, after the Nazis came to power, Hermann Göring officially decreed its closure, referring to the Bauhaus as a den of communist spies and a center for the dissemination of "degenerate" art. It is said that when a representative of the Gestapo summoned Mies Van Der Rohe, the last director, to his office, he told him: *Bauhaus is an idea and has nothing to do with politics. Look at your desk, your horrible desk. Do you like it? I would throw it out the window.*" Nazism put an end to a unique and irreplaceable design school in the world.

## The Style

**1920** Nel 1917, in the Netherlands, a movement called Neoplasticism was founded with the publication of the magazine De Stijl, although initially it remained limited to the Dutch art world. The magazine boasted several prominent names, the most well-known being the Dutch painter Piet Mondrian, a leading proponent of the movement's ideas.

The highest expression of De Stijl architecture can be found in the work of Gerrit Thomas Rietveld, who was initially a cabinetmaker but later became a craftsman and designer, joining the movement two years later in 1919.

Rietveld was the son of a carpenter and learned the trade from his father at a young age before opening his own workshop in 1917. In his early years of involvement with the movement, he created the Red and Blue Chair, which embodied the principles of De Stijl in its design and form.

The chair was originally made of beechwood in 1917 but acquired its famous multicolored appearance in 1923 when Piet Mondrian added the characteristic red and blue colors. The abstract composition formed by simple geometric elements represented the desire to reduce form to its essential elements. It can be said that in this chair, design served the purpose of mass production. There is one more observation to make—the rigid seating allows for relaxation but not for sleeping. According to Rietveld, this was intentional to emphasize the awakening of consciousness. The chair is ideal for reading or meditation.

Rietveld's ideas also stemmed from the belief that furniture of the time was too heavy and bulky. For this reason, he revolutionized the design and production process by creating simple and accessible models for everyone.

Rietveld nurtured a dream of democratic design combined with large-scale production of his creations, which only came to fruition after his death when his heirs granted Cassina the rights to produce the furniture conceived by his creative mind.

## Aerodynamism

**1920** In 1929, a economic crisis occurred in the United States that had the power to disrupt the global economy. Its effects were devastating, resulting in increased layoffs and subsequent impoverishment of the population. With limited money, people had no desire to make purchases, posing a significant challenge for the industry. In response, the industry sought the assistance of graphic designers to redesign objects and make them appealing to the general public.

Towards the late 1920s, a new generation of designers emerged on the American scene. Each of them came from a different cultural background, which led to a richness in expressive terms. However, they all agreed that Design was essential not only on an industrial level but also in commerce.

After the major crisis of '29, their conception of products had the potential to revive the manufacturing sector. Aerodynamics, with the recent invention of the wind tunnel, became a part of Design and revolutionized everything. Objects increasingly resembled torpedoes, and monobloc shapes, streamlined in metal with rounded corners, started to appear. This trend extended to the curving of building walls and everyday objects, as everything sought to express concepts of strength and speed. These new forms originated from the pens of these designers, inspired by Hollywood advertising and the facades of Las Vegas.

People soon began to love this streamlined style, which aimed to achieve greater speed through its curved shapes, thus distancing itself from any possible crisis. Bel Geddes, Dreyfuss, and Loewy were the prominent figures associated with this Design. These years witnessed the birth of Streamlining, one of the most significant phenomena in the history of American Design. It rejected Rationalism and instead proposed symbols and a parsimonious use of decorative elements that were integrated into the very structure of the objects.

Due to the war, this phenomenon had a short lifespan, but its influence is still perceived today.

Regardless of the passage of a century, certain objects are unforgettable, leaving behind a trail of their presence everywhere.


## North wind

**1930** During the 1920s, Scandinavian design emerged in Denmark, Finland, Sweden, Norway, and Iceland. These countries share a common culture, economy, and roots, and each of them celebrates Scandinavian furniture design with a clear naturalistic correlation. The Scandinavian style is undoubtedly essential, bright, and deeply rooted in the natural context. The lines are simple and stylized, and every element has a practical function in this style. However, this simplicity should not lead us to believe that the design is neglected because the opposite is true.

The lines are carefully studied for their beauty, and even the choice of colors is not random. Since there are few daylight hours, white or light colors are preferred for the walls to reflect the limited light. Often, these light shades are also used for furniture to meet the same need.

Scandinavian furniture was designed by its creators following the values of ethics and morality. These nations have always placed great importance on family and home.

One of the major exponents of this style was Alvar Aalto, who interpreted this philosophy as a propensity for balance. He founded the furniture company Artek with his first wife and worked as a designer, architect, and university professor. One of his most famous projects was the Paimio Sanatorium in Finland, which he completed in 1928. In this work, he focused on modulating light to make the stay for patients more pleasant.

For Alvar, architecture should correspond to a social art that serves human needs. One of these needs is undoubtedly light, which influences people's moods.

To complete the sanatorium project, he also designed furniture pieces such as the Paimio Chair 41, which is still produced today. Suspended on the frame in only four points, the seat remains floating, offering great elasticity and functionality.


## Organic

**1940** When we talk about Organic Design, we refer to nature, which has always been considered the best designer. Organic Design highlights the extraordinary design economy of natural elements, which possess functionality and aesthetic sensibility. Designers, together with architects, draw inspiration from these natural elements, particularly their structure. In 1940, the MoMa (Museum of Modern Art) organized a competition inviting designers to create furniture, textiles, and lamps in "Organic Design." The curator, Elliot Noyes, described the event as the "harmonious organization of parts within the whole, according to structure, material, and purpose." The winners were awarded production contracts and the honor of having their work exhibited. Not everyone knows that this exhibition introduced Eero Saarinen and Charles Eames to the world, who, along with their team, won for the creation of the Organic Chair.

Extensive research on form and materials, conducted by numerous industry professionals, resulted in the birth of numerous design icons produced between the 1930s and 1950s. Some of these creations have been produced more recently, thanks to technological advancements that made them possible.

The organic movement can be considered an evolution of the Art Nouveau style, as both movements draw inspiration from nature, although in organic design, the forms tend to become purer.

During these years, countless ideas came to life, mostly driven by the need for well-being combined with a more humanistic approach. This type of design has never experienced a true decline but has gained renewed popularity over the years, thanks to the creative ideas of designers who have reinvented objects through new lines.

The development of new technologies has allowed for the exploration of these curved lines. In this regard, I recall the works of Ross Lovegrove, whose creations are naturally ethereal and should not be overlooked.


## Classical Italian

**1950** If we consider Europe, the art of design had already established itself long ago, but it took some time for it to conquer the scene in our beautiful country, also due to the extremely fragmented geopolitical landscape.

In the 19th century, Italy was primarily an agricultural country at the dawn of 1860. Enlightened patrons who understood the importance of the historical moment embraced groups of architects and artists under their protective wings.

The end of the century witnessed the birth of Italian companies that would make history not only in our country. Pirelli, a leader in tire manufacturing, was founded in 1872, while Richard Ginori, specialized in ceramics production, was established in 1880.

1890 marked the year of Fiat's establishment. This was followed by Olivetti, Necchi, Piaggio, Magneti Marelli, and many others. Around the figure of Margherita Sarfatti, a personality very close to Benito Mussolini, and her cultural salon, the "Gruppo Novecento" (Group of the Twentieth Century) was born in Milan in 1922. The key idea was to create a movement that opposed Futurism.

The artists and architects who participated in this movement appealed to classical culture, with architecture based on principles of solidity, harmony, and order.

In 1928, the first Italian architecture magazine, Domus, was launched under the direction of Giò Ponti. It criticized, informed, and proposed innovative ideas to the general public.

In 1946, an innovative exhibition called RIMA (Italian Meeting for Furniture Exhibitions) was organized by the Milan Triennale. It gave emerging young architects the opportunity to showcase their designs for individual furniture pieces and/or standard housing units. Furniture designs that could be mass-produced and specifically designed for small spaces were proposed. This was how every square centimeter began to be rationalized and utilized.
From this point on, Italian design became a symbol of excellence and a point of reference to the extent that collectors and museums competed to possess creations from the 1950s.
Giò Ponti, Ico Parisi, Ignazio Gardella, Franco Albini, Carlo Mollino, and many others were Italian architects who promoted the sober and elegant style that would find its way into the hearts and homes of Italians.
The 1950s also marked the boom of household appliances: refrigerators, televisions, vacuum cleaners, washing machines, lamps, and other modern and minimalistic furniture objects became increasingly present in homes.
Although Italian design exhibitions were inaugurated in many world capitals after the mid-1950s, the reference point continued to be the Milan Triennale, which reached its tenth edition in 1954.
In 1954, the Compasso D'Oro award was also established. Promoted by La Rinascente, the first edition saw fifteen designers triumph: Bruno Munari, Gino Sarfatti, and Marcello Nizzoli with his innovative Olivetti Lettera 22 typewriter.
The 1960s marked further development in Italian design, thanks to the use of new materials such as foam rubber, polyurethane, and plastic. From this point on, industrial design would undergo a definitive transformation.

## Counter-Design

**1960** The 1960s marked the birth of the so-called Radical Design (also known as Anti-Design or Contro-Design), which had its heart in Florence. Originating from groups of designers such as Archizoom and Superstudio, it quickly spread to Milan, Europe, and the rest of the world, where it became known as Italian Radical Design.

This movement emerged from the ideology of young designers who opposed the rigidity and sobriety of the classical style, aligning themselves with the political and student movements of 1968. The definitive break with the past marked the beginning of what is called "Emotional Design."

The primary goal of these young designers and aspiring architects, driven by political fervor, was to create unconventional, irreverent, ironic, eccentric, and innovative objects in both form and function. Elegance and functionality were swept away by irreverence and non-functionality, resulting in controversial objects capable of eliciting waves of passion and emotion through their sensationalism.

The underlying idea of Contro-Design is the same as that of the visual arts: to create new stimuli through novelty and provocation. Objects were loaded with provocative meanings, as they aimed to represent poetic and artistic creations detached from any functionality. Examples of this movement include kneeling tables, unusable furniture, bed frames with nails, and wobbly chairs – purely decorative objects.

One of the central figures of Contro-Design was Leonardo Savioli, a professor of Architecture at the University of Florence, who encouraged his students to experiment and embrace radical lifestyles. Contro-Design officially originated in Pistoia in 1966 with the manifesto and the exhibition titled "Superarchitettura." Studio 65, Ufo, and Zigurat are just a few of the protagonists of this movement, which finds its roots in student movements, political struggles, rock 'n' roll, Pop Art, and Space Design.

Although Contro-Design represented only a short-lived burst that faded after about a decade, its contribution was crucial to the development of emotional design, which spread worldwide between 1960 and 1970.


## Pragmatism

**1970** The situation in Germany was quite different. Due to the Nazi regime, Germany not only lost the Second World War but also found itself completely divided, with its eastern part under Russian domination, which imposed socialist policies. The Design of the German Democratic Republic (GDR, also known as East Germany) was profoundly influenced by the country's geopolitical situation, as it was isolated from the rest of the world for over four decades.

The design production during those years was characterized by a lack of quality, a subdued and outdated aesthetic, and outdated technology. Following the fall of the Berlin Wall in 1989, the Soviet influence (along with its production) disappeared, only to reappear on the scene about sixty years later with wonderful objects that interested only the most nostalgic collectors.

The Habernoll gallery in Dreieich inaugurated an exhibition called "The Beautiful Uniform Design" with the primary purpose of showcasing products from the GDR.

This allowed West Germany to become acquainted with the culture that effectively belonged to a foreign country but also confronted the post-war reality. With the monetary reunification in June 1990, products from East Germany (such as Trabants, Juwel cigarettes, Club-Cola, and Spee soap) competed with products from West Germany (such as Golf cars, Camel cigarettes, Coca-Cola, and Ariel detergent).

However, this challenge was short-lived because the poor quality and outdated forms contributed to making East German products mere relics of a bygone socio-economic system. It marked the end of the German Democratic Republic and Russian supremacy.

## Color and Bolides

**1980** In the 1980s, a new group emerged on the design scene: we're talking about the Memphis Group, which began to attract attention with its use of colors and geometric shapes. Founded by Ettore Sottsass in 1981 in Milan, the group consisted of international architects and designers. The idea behind the group was to break free from marketing offices and industrial constraints, designing whatever they desired without adhering to rules: in a sense, the project aimed to continue what had been done by Studio Alchimia.

It was a true cultural phenomenon that deliberately positioned itself outside the boundaries of good taste. The group's first collection was absolutely innovative: the use of materials like plastic laminate, which was considered "cheap," vibrant colors, exuberant motifs, stacked geometric forms resembling totems, and asymmetries were the main ingredients.

Memphis creations undoubtedly carried a strong emotional and creative charge, but they were practically unusable, which is why they represented the "manifesto" of anti-design. In the Memphis Group's philosophy, all objects were supposed to have a dual function: a technical one and an expressive one, almost sculptural. For example, taking a chair as an example, when it's not being used by anyone, its primary function is to be an object in the environment.

Due to commercial failure, Sottsass considered the group's experience concluded in 1985, but a sacrilegious creativity remained. In 1986, the Bolidists group was founded, distinguished by the dynamism of forms derived from futurism, American influences, comics, and research on 1930s architecture.

The Bolidists represented the natural evolution of the Alchimia and Memphis Group experiences. They managed to capture the attention of media in culture, current affairs, and fashion during the triennium of 1986-1989. Their works were cited and published in international and Italian magazines, which is why the Bolidists are considered a reference point.

The Bolidist movement was able to anticipate the arrival of the Internet and the development of new communication methods with a lead time of about 15 years, speaking of simultaneity and a fluid city, a place of contact without physical limits.
Design flourished in the city of Milan, making it a true hub of international interest.

## Play Design
**1990** The 1990s represent a turning point in the world of design, characterized by the triumph of provocative objects that are positively received by the market. During this period, design evolves, freeing itself from the ideological implications that had characterized the previous two decades. Technological innovations and new materials offer endless creative possibilities, pushing design to surpass traditional boundaries and experiment with new expressive forms.
The fundamental form-function relationship that had characterized design for decades begins to lose value, and design moves in a fluid manner, without a specific goal or direction. This period marks the emergence of designers who stand out for their ability to break the mold, transgress conventions, and create objects that evoke wonder and interest.
Among the most influential designers of this period, we find Philippe Starck, Karim Rashid, and Ron Arad. They draw extensively from Italian Radical Design, reinterpreting it and projecting it towards the future. Their creations stand out for their bold forms, the use of innovative materials, and the ability to communicate a strong and distinctive message.
As mentioned, during this period, the product loses its practical function to assume an iconoclastic function. Aesthetics become predominant, and design objects become true works of art. Forms become explicit, somewhat contorted, and at times exuberant, while functionality takes a back seat. This new approach to design opens the doors to new creative possibilities, allowing designers to explore uncharted territories

and create unique and surprising objects.

However, not all design objects follow this trend. In some cases, even in a functional design object, significant imagination may be required to understand a particular form. This demonstrates that design is a complex process in which every design choice is the result of a series of considerations and evaluations. There is no right or wrong form for an object, but rather a form that responds to the needs and intentions of the designer.

During the 1990s, there is also an economic crisis that impacts the design industry. In response to this situation, there is a trend towards a more stripped-down, minimalist, and essential design. The concept of minimalism becomes predominant, with a reduction of superfluous elements and an emphasis on the purity of forms and lines.

At the same time, environmental issues begin to gain importance in the world of design. Awareness of the environmental impact of industrial production spreads, and ecology and recycling start being discussed. These themes become integral parts of the design process, with the goal of creating sustainable and environmentally friendly objects.

In this context, the movement of Droog Design emerges, a Dutch network that proposes a "non-design" approach. Their aim is to rebel against the conventional idea of form and function, proposing objects that stand out for their simplicity and humor. Droog Design projects are based on the use of common and recycled materials, combined with a straightforward mindset.

This alternative approach to design becomes very popular, especially among young audiences who seek affordably priced and often self-produced objects.

Ecology and industry, however, travel on parallel tracks, and often Droog Design products are incompatible with large-scale industrial production. Nevertheless, the movement has contributed to redefining the aesthetics of design, introducing a new approach and language that resonated with an

audience and industry tired of refinement and decoration.
During the 1990s, the emergence of "Play Design" also takes place, which will have a significant impact on the design scene for the next three decades. This approach emphasizes the playful and interactive aspect of design objects, seeking to emotionally engage users. An emblematic example of this trend is represented by the company Alessi, which in 1991 decided to completely innovate its product line.

Based on pedagogical studies, Alessi realizes that customers need objects that go beyond mere functionality and are capable of conveying emotions and feelings. Thus, the "Family Follows Fiction" product line is born, characterized by anthropomorphic objects that evoke human emotions and relationships.

These objects communicate five different types of messages: maternal, paternal, childlike, related to life and death, and eros-related. Alessi's goal is to create objects that can become part of people's lives, becoming faithful companions and sources of inspiration.

In conclusion, the 1990s were a period of great ferment in the world of design. New trends and approaches redefined the very concept of design, leading to a blend of art and functionality.

Formal experimentation, the use of innovative materials, and the search for new creative expressions characterized this period. Design objects became vehicles for conveying emotions, stimulating curiosity, and evoking wonder in the audience. Childhood memories and experiences also played a significant role during this period. Sales skyrocketed, and the line was copied by other companies.

The underlying idea is that every object has an emotional value first and foremost: purchases are often dictated by emotional significance rather than the mere function performed by the object. The feeling of well-being generated in the customer was the basis of the success of this trend.

## Liquid Design

**2000** The products of the end of the millennium are mainly characterized by a lack of substance, and their creation is marked by a lack of original ideas. Design becomes purely a commercial product, and the artists of the time create objects whose categorical imperative is to be excessive and extravagant in order to attract marketing attention.
Dieter Rams, one of the greatest designers in modern history, expressed his personal (critical) opinion by using the Chair-One outdoor chair by Konstantin Grcic as an example. The chair is visually appealing and highly functional, but Rams commented, "It's very beautiful and made of top-quality materials... but if you place it in the garden under the sun during the summer and then sit on it, you'll end up with an unwanted hot tattoo on your back."
The real problem lies in the fact that these objects have a purely aesthetic function and lack the innovation that is the foundation of the art of Design. The new century marks a true turning point: designers seek the right balance between aesthetics and functionality. They draw inspiration from Radical Design, embracing the idea of exciting and innovative forms while avoiding the excesses and extravagances of the '60s and '70s. The tones of these creations are never exaggerated; they embody a sovereign equilibrium that doesn't strive desperately for innovation and extravagance.
Liquid Design is characterized by a certain irony, and its creations are fluid, instantaneous, and, above all, born to "exist" rather than to "appear" or to simply "do." With the technological revolution, objects begin to communicate with each other, and new control methodologies are invented. Additionally, while eco-friendly solutions started to be discussed towards the end of the millennium, the "Green" aspect becomes almost a categorical imperative, even though it often remains merely superficial.

## Form Fiction

**2010** The first ten years of the new millennium quickly take a wrong direction: products move away from their cultural roots and reality, being characterized only by a strong aesthetic exuberance. Both clothing and furniture items are recognized solely based on their association with a particular brand/designer that is popular at the time of their release in the market.

Once again, the problem lies in the ephemeral story that brand/designer tells, the lack of substance, and the mere commercial gimmick that serves the sole purpose of selling. From Milan to New York, passing through Paris and London, creations are increasingly detached from their functionality and destined to exist only on some online platforms that falsely present them as culture, when they are not: they won't become part of everyday life.

Design begins to represent the pairing of form/fiction (opposite to the form/function pairing that should be the foundation). Objects increasingly lean towards appearance, towards a self-referential aesthetic function, turning design from being project-oriented to virtual.

However, if the public massively embraces well-designed objects, it is also thanks to technological innovations. Liquid crystal displays or carbon fiber (which simultaneously provide strength and lightness) play a role. LED technology, which completely revolutionizes domestic lighting, starts to become accessible to a larger number of people.

Design thus shifts towards a technological direction that allows perfect blends of functionality and innovation.

## Go beyond

**2020** Although buying objects is an essential action and stopping it is unthinkable (especially nowadays), especially in recent decades, this action is carried out in an almost compulsive manner. The phenomenon that is spreading more and more is that of unconscious shopping. When did we start giving in to the impulse of buying just for the sake of it? The answer is simple. We live in a world where buying and owning new objects hold greater value because the logic of capitalism considers selling to be more important than repairing, and objects are built to last only a certain number of years. The competition is ruthless, and there is an imperative to always be fashionable and continuously design new models (whether it's refrigerators, cell phones, or sofas) to offer in the market.
This phenomenon is called "planned obsolescence": objects break (they are programmed to do so), money is not spent on repairing them, but instead, they are discarded and replaced with new ones. This fuels a harmful vicious circle for our planet as we are completely overwhelmed by all types of waste. The sole purpose is consumption, without caring about anything else. It is precisely because of this global emergency that Design is trying to serve for improvement by proposing a rethinking of spaces and objects. One of the oldest functions of Design is, in fact, linked to utility: designing and constructing not only objects but also spaces and services is essential to bring improvement to human life. The history of Design shows how the most free creative process has then shifted towards a more utility-oriented direction: thanks to technology as well, Design has fully served the changes and needs of society.
Starting from the industrial revolution, it is nearly impossible to keep track of every single change that has accompanied the growth of the Design phenomenon until its establishment as an autonomous discipline in the 20th century.

From that moment on, each decade has been crucial as it has given Design a new aspect (ergonomics, planning, computing, role in society) and contributed to creating internal branches within the discipline, giving rise to various fields: interior design, product design, experience design, visual design. Just as the digital revolution was gaining more ground, the emergency caused by the Covid-19 pandemic pushed designers to rethink the boundaries of a world that was drastically changing around us. Remote work and new social habits are now part of a world that is no longer the same as a few years ago. This is the greatest challenge for designers who are trying to use their creativity to design a world with new spaces, new distances, and new habits.

Thanks to the increasing development of technology, particularly 3D printing, it is highly likely that in the near future, designers will build objects tailored to the consumer. In this way, the distance between the two parties is greatly reduced. The designed object can be changed not only in color and shape but in its most intimate nature. This will lead to infinite customizable collections, and customers will receive the requested product in very short periods. The future of design is intrinsically linked to the evolution of our society. As the world moves into the unknown, it is difficult to predict with certainty which direction design will take. However, one thing is certain: design is adaptable, it adjusts and transforms based on the needs and values of the society in which it operates.

## The future

It is important to recognize that the problem with objects is not only about companies and designers but also involves consumers. We are often too focused on our specific roles and fail to consider the consequences of our purchasing behavior. Compulsive buying of unnecessary objects contributes to the accumulation of superfluous goods and the depletion of the planet's resources.

Addressing this phenomenon requires a change in mindset from consumers. It is essential to develop critical awareness regarding our purchases and their consequences. We must consider the real value of the objects we buy, beyond their functionality or aesthetic impact. We should ask ourselves if we truly need them and if they contribute to our well-being and that of the planet.

Education and awareness are powerful tools for promoting a culture of conscious consumption. It is important to inform consumers about the negative effects of impulsive buying and support sustainable alternatives such as recycling, reusing, and waste reduction.

Additionally, greater attention needs to be given to the production and management of objects. Companies and young designers must take responsibility for creating sustainable products by using eco-friendly materials, reducing waste, and promoting durability and reparability. Objects should be a resource for people, companies, and the planet. This calls for an integrated approach involving both design and production.

This implies that designers must carefully consider the materials used and ensure they are durable and easy to repair. For example, using screws instead of glue for assembly could simplify the repair process. Furthermore, designers should create modular products so that damaged parts can be easily replaced without having to replace the entire object.

Concurrently, companies need to adopt a mindset that facilitates reparability. They should provide efficient repair and support services, equipping users with the necessary information to extend the operational life of an object.

Addressing this issue requires a significant but achievable cultural, industrial, and educational change. A new attitude can help reduce waste, prolong the useful life of objects, and promote greater environmental sustainability.

Ultimately, the future of our planet depends on all of us. Now more than ever, it is necessary to adopt a responsible and conscious approach to consumption, considering the social and environmental implications of our behaviors. Only by doing so can we contribute to reducing the negative impact of objects on our lives and the planet, promoting sustainable design that respects our current and future needs.

**Pouf "The End"**
GUFRAM

# BIBLIOGRAPHY


| AUTORE | TITOLO | EDITORE |
| --- | --- | --- |
| Giulio Iacchetti, | 20 oggetti a reazione poetica | Editrice Compositori |
| Paola Antonelli, | Achille Castiglioni | Corraini Edizioni |
| Frida Doveil | Aldo Cibic | Abitare Segesta |
| Beppe Finessi | Alessandro Mendini | Corraini Edizioni |
| Roberto Borghi | Andrea Branzi. Oggetti e territori | Silvana editoriale |
| Beppe Finessi | Angelo Mangiarotti: Scolpire/Costruire | Corraini Edizioni |
| Claudia Donà | Anna Castelli Ferrieri. Architecture and | FAAR Foundation |
| anty pansera | antonia campi | Silvana Editoriale |
| Anty Pansera | Antonia Campi. Creatività, forma e | Silvana editoriale |
| Antonio Citterio and | Antonio Citterio | Antonio Citterio and |
| Alba Cappellieri | Antonio Citterio. Architettura e design | Skira |
| Grande Valentina | Bauhaus.L'idea che cambiò il mondo. | Centauria |
| Beppe Finessi | Bruno Munari | Silvana editoriale |
| branzi andrea | capire il design | Giunti |
| Pasca Vanni | Christopher Dresser | Lupetti |
| Whiteway michael | Christopher Dresser 1834-1904 | Skira |
| bruno munari | da cosa nasce cosa | Editori Laterza |
| Hohne Gunter | ddr design | Komet |
| trabucco francesco | design | Bollati |
| Bassi alberto | design | Il Mulino |
| Alessi Alberto | design anonimo in italia | Mondadori |
| godau marian | design germania | Rizzoli |
| Stefano Casciani | Design in Italia 1950-90 | Politi Editore |
| Achille Castiglioni | Design Interview: Achille Castiglioni | Corraini, Museo |
| Ettore Sottsass | Design Interview: Ettore Sottsass | Corraini, Museo |
| Richard Sapper | Design Interview: Richard Sapper | Corraini, Museo |
| neumann claudia | design italia | Rizzoli |
| renato minetto | design italiano nei musei del mondo | Sacs |
| branzi/de lucchi | design italliano degli anni 50 | RDE |
| Bassi alberto | design Ontemporaneo | Il Mulino |
| Giannin Anna Maria | Design Percezione visiva e cognizione | Giunti |
| Alessi chiara | design senza designer | Edizioni Laterza |
| Martinuz Martino | Design Tecnologia | Lettera 22 |
| gentil enzo biffi | design una storia italiana | Meet Design |
| Corrado Maurizio | Design. Una storia sbagliata | Armillaria |
| caffarelli Michele | Didesign. Ovvero niente. | Espresso Edizioni |
| Maldonado Tomás | Disegno industriale un riesame | Feltrinelli |
| Pasca Vanni | Dresser il primo industrial designer | Lupetti |
| fuad-luke alastair | eco design | Logos |
| Norman Donald | Emotionl Design | Apogeo |
| Beatrice Mascellani | Ettore Sottsass: vorrei sapere perché | Electa |
| yudina anna | furni tecture | L'Ippocampo |
| Daniel Kelly | gino sarfatti il design della luce | Triennale Milano |
| Laura Falconi | Gio Ponti. Interni, oggetti, disegni 1920- | Electa |
| hohenegger alfred | graphic design | Romana Libri |
| Vari | Ho visto cose... | Bur |
| Rashid Karim | I Want to Change the World Book Case | Edizione speciale |
| Mancini Giovanna | Icone. Mito storie e personaggi | Luiss |
| Bassi alberto | Il design anonimo in Italia | Electa |

| Scodeller  Dario | Il design dei Castiglioni | Corraini Edizioni |
|---|---|---|
| sarfatti gino | il design della luce | Triennale Milano |
| Novembre  Fabio | Il Design spiegato a mia madre | Rizzoli |
| Bellini Mario | Il design spiegato ai bambini | Bompiani |
| gregotti vittorio | il disegno del prodotto industriale | Electa |
| dario russo | il lato oscuro del design | Lupetti |
| Bramston David | Il linguaggio dei prodotti | Zanichelli |
| sudjic deyan | il linguaggio delle cose | Editori Laterza |
| polato pietro | il modello del design | Hoepli |
| Giampiero Bosoni | Il Modo Italiano. Design e avanguardia nel | Skira |
| lakshmi bhaskaram | il tempo del design | Logos |
| heskett john | industrial design | Rusconi |
| dorfles gillo | Introduzione al disegno industriale | Einaudi |
| Dorfles Gillo | Kitsch: The World of Bad Taste | Mazzotta |
| donald norman | la caffettiera del masochista | Giunti |
| arnaboldi mario | la disciplina del progetto | Clup |
| Alessi Alberto | La Fabbrica dei sogni | Rizzoli |
| Castelli Giulio | La Fabbrica del design | Skira |
| triennale | la lingua degli specchi | Electa |
| shijders c.j. | la sezione aurea | Franco Muzzio |
| dardi domitila | lampade | Motta Architettura |
| masini lara/vinca | l'arte del novecento | Giunti |
| Alessi chiara | le caffettiere dei miei bisnonni | Utet |
| gramigna giuliana | le fabbriche del design | Umberto Allemandi |
| d ascanio corradino | le macchine volanti | Giorgetti |
| cecchini cecilia | le parole del design | List |
| Dario Scodeller | Livio e Piero Castiglioni. Il progetto della | Electa |
| bonami francesco | lo potevo fare anch'io | Mondadori |
| wilhide elizabeth | luci d'arredo | Logos |
| Decelle Philippe | L'Utopie du Tout Plastique 1960-1973 | Fondation pour |
| Francesco Zurlo | Makio Hasuike | Abitare Segesta |
| Cinzia Ferrara | Marc Newson. Design tra organicità e | Lupetti |
| Aldo Colonnetti | Massimo Iosa Ghini. Da designer ad | Editrice Compositori |
| vari vari | materials matters v | Material Connection |
| Fiorella Bulegato, | Michele De Lucchi. Comincia qui e finisce là | Electa |
| Boym Constantin | New Russian Design | Rizzoli |
| De Fusco  Renato | Parodie del Design | Umberto Allemandi |
| kanizska legrenzi | percezione,linguaggio,pensiero | Il Mulino |
| Beppe Finessi | Pio Manzù. Quando il mondo era moderno | Electa |
| Lidwell William | Principi universali di design | Logos |
| thompson rob | product and furniture design | Thames & Hudson |
| Bonetto Marco | Rodolfo Bonetto Industrial Designer | Fondazione Manzoni |
| Alba Cappellieri | Ron Arad | Mondadori Arte |
| Lovegrove Ross | Ross Lovegrove | Sieveking |
| bertolino giorgina | saper vedere i movimenti artistici | Mondadori |
| Ghidelli Giacomo | Senza titoli nella storia del design | Libraccio Editore |
| Cristina Morozzi | Stefano Giovannoni | Mondadori Arte |
| de fusco renato | storia del design | Editori Laterza |
| d'amato  gabriella | Storia del Design | Mondadori |
| Alessi alberto | the dream factory | Zuffi |

# Author

*Since my childhood, I have been driven by a deep curiosity and the aspiration to build with my own hands what I lacked.*
*This desire not only nurtured my growth but also propelled me to bring to life what does not yet exist, guiding me on a path toward new, bold explorations in the incredible world of objects.*

 matteobianchi.it

 #matteobianchi.it

# Acknowledgements

This book came to life thanks to a moment of inspiration with
my daughter Marta, who one evening enlightened me with
these words:

"Dad, the stories you tell are very beautiful;
you should write them down."

It was that spark that brought this book to life.

My gratitude also goes to my wife Erika,
whose trust and support have turned moments
of doubt into opportunities for growth.

If you notice any errors or inaccuracies while reading this book, I would be grateful if you could kindly report them. Your feedback is valuable for improving the quality of the text. Thank you in advance for your contribution.

oggettario@gmail.com

www.ingramcontent.com/pod-product-compliance
Lightning Source LLC
Chambersburg PA
CBHW051050250726
48656CB00001B/233